STORIES, TALES, YARNS, VIGNETTES, ANECDOTES AND MEMENTOES
TO
BOGGLE YOUR BRAIN,
MUDDLE YOUR MIND
AND
CRAM YOUR CRANIUM

BY

GILBERT W. DAVIES

COMPUTERIZED AND EDITED BY

FLORICE M. FRANK

HiStory ink Books
P. O. Box 52
Hat Creek, CA 96040

ISBN: 1-887200-12-6

Printed in the United States of America by
Maverick Publications, Bend, Oregon
www.maverickbooks.com

INTRODUCTION

These stories, facts and figures are not new. Your author spent hundreds of hours researching the information in the 1960s and 1970s as chapter introductions to five of his books published by three New York firms: Funk & Wagnalls, A. S. Barnes and Company and Drake Publishers Inc.

The subjects were as far reaching as the number of chapters in the collection. One book related to Geography, one to Sports and one to the Arts. The other two contained general topics. Since the books are out of print we thought it would be fun to resurrect a few of the more fascinating and informative introductions.

GWD & FMF

TABLE OF CONTENTS

ANIMALS AND PLANTS

ANIMALS

A DOG'S LIFE

One dog who would have never won a dog show, but traveled around the world, was given countless awards—among them a medal of honor by the Japanese emperor--and became the special friend of postal clerks all over the United States, was called Owney. He was a little dog of uncertain parentage who, in the winter of 1888, wandered into the post office at Albany, New York, cuddled up on a pile of warm mailbags and went to sleep.

His first trips were to New York City. This developed the gypsy in him and he started on a tour of America. Up and down and across the country he went, happy to be with his dearest friends, the postal clerks, who regarded it as an honor to have Owney as their guest. To the dog's collar were attached tags, medals, inscriptions, and post-office marks from nearly every state in the Union until a special harness had to be made for them. He visited Mexico, Canada and was given a great ovation in China. At the end of his glo-wide travels Owney was given a reception and a silver medal on which were inscribed, "The Greatest Dog Traveler in the World." When Owney died, his body was mounted and, together with all his decorations, placed in the Smithsonian Institution.

THE CAMEL CAPER

Jefferson Davis touched off a United States camel caper when, as secretary of war, he was faced with serious transportation problems during the 1840s because of rapid territorial expansion. Davis proposed that the army use camels to transport men, mail, and material; help fight Indians; and hasten the settlement of the new land. He argued that the Southwest was similar in geography to the Near East, where camels had been the major form of transportation since biblical times. With the idea that camels could be introduced, Congress appropriated $30,000 in 1855 to get the great camel experiment under way.

Two young officers, Army Major Henry C. Wayne and Navy Lieutenant David D. Porter, were dispatched to Egypt and Asia on a camel-buying mission. The officers soon learned about the ins-and-outs of camel trading. They finally loaded their ship with 33 one-humped camels, purchased for approximately $250 each. Birth increased the lot to 34 by the time the ship landed at Indianaola, Texas on May 14, 1856. A year later 41 more camels arrived. The animals were kept near San Antonio, Texas and at first were used to carry supplies and equipment between army posts. From there they were removed to

Camp Verde, about 60 miles southwest of San Antonio, where a permanent camel post was located.

It was found that the camels could easily carry 600 pounds each, cover 30 to 40 miles a day, climb mountain trails, feed on plants and prickly cacti that no other animal would eat, and go without water for six to ten days. Camel caravans were sent to Fort Tejon, California and made several pack trips between there and Albuquerque, New Mexico.

The camels' army caretakers disliked them, however, as did the transportation mainstays of the Southwest, horses and mules. Furthermore, camels were useless in fighting Indians because of their unimpressive 2-miles per hour gait.

At the outbreak of the Civil War the great experiment was discontinued. Some of the camels were sold at auction and ended up in zoos and circuses. Part of the herd, however, wandered off into the Arizona desert.

RATTLE, BUZZ OR HISS

It is widely believed that rattlesnakes always rattle before they strike, that they can't climb over a wall of cactus, and that whiskey is helpful in treating snakebite. As it happens, these and many other ideas about rattlesnakes are untrue.

Rattlesnakes can be encountered at almost any altitude. Most people don't expect to find them at altitudes over 6,000 feet, but in the southwestern United States they have been encountered as high as the 11,000 foot level, and in Mexico up to 14,000 feet. In most parts of the country rattlesnakes hibernate in dens in the winter, but they are generally in the open from March or April to October or December, depending on local climate and weather conditions.

The most distinctive feature of the rattlesnake is its rattle, which it vibrates when it is disturbed or annoyed. The actual sound is a kind of toneless buzz or hiss, which is sometimes confused with the sound made by the cicada. Although it was once supposed that these snakes acquired one new rattle each year, it has now been established that they get a new one each time that they shed their skins, which may be from one to four times a year, depending on age, species and climate.

There are some 30 different kinds of rattlesnakes in the United States, and they vary in size, markings and coloration. Neither large nor small rattlesnakes have the ability to travel rapidly over the ground, which is so often attributed to them in legend. Far from being able to keep up with a galloping horse, they can't even match the speed of a man in any kind of a hurry. The rattler's strike, on the other hand, is a rapid motion, so fast that the reptile's head cannot be followed by the human eye. At the end of the strike the rattler's mouth is wide open, with the fangs in the upper jaw swung forward to pierce whatever is struck.

Judged purely on mortality statistics, rattlesnakes offer no outstanding hazard to man. The number of people killed in the United States every year does not exceed 30 or 35, which is less than the number killed annually by lightning.

THE INSECTS

Insects are curious, little beasts, the oldest on earth. They have skittered and bussed around for some 300 million years, and today, despite poisons and flyswatters, they still number nine out of every ten of the earth's creatures. Given its way, the insect would steal man's food and fiber and endanger his health. But man has attempted to control the insect, largely with the use of poisons.

Now man has chosen to set aside his strongest weapons – the persistent pesticides such as DDT, so once again he is faced with wormy apples and crop diseases. Man has employed every possible means of overkill from the heel of his boot to the flat of his hand, from aircraft to sound effects. But the odds, as always, are with the bugs. Take two houseflies, for instance. If they and their progeny bred successfully, they would produce 190 quintillion flies in just four months. Of course, birds, disease and other natural enemies keep this from happening. Or take a flight of locusts attacking a wheat field. They might weigh as much as 50,000 tons, the combined weight of 250 B-52 jet bombers loaded for war, and in a single day they would eat their own weight in wheat – enough to feed 5 million human beings.

A BIRD'S LIFE

There are several theories as to why birds migrate. One is that in earlier ages nonmigratory birds swarmed over the entire Northern Hemisphere, which at that time afforded a plentiful year-long food supply, such as now exists only in the tropics. Gradually, however, the glacial ice fields pushed southward, forcing the birds before them until finally all bird life was concentrated in the southern latitudes. As ages passed, the ice cap gradually retreated and each spring the birds whose ancestral home had formerly been in the North tried to return there, only to be driven south again at the approach of winter. As the size of the ice-covered area decreased, the journeys northward became longer. Eventually the climatic conditions of our present age were established and the birds continue the habit of migration, flying north in the summer to raise their young and returning to the southland when winter has cut off their food supply.

An opposing theory proposes that the ancestral home of all birds was in the tropics and that as this area became overpopulated, many species were gradually forced northward to find food and breeding grounds, only to be forced southward again by the annual recurrence of winter. Gradually, as the glacial ice retreated, vast areas of virgin country became suitable for summer occupancy, but the winter habitat in the South remained the home in which the birds returned after the nesting season.

Both of these theories assume that migration is an ingrained habit; but, both have been criticized on biological and geological grounds, so neither should be accepted without qualification.

THE STUBBORN LEMMINGS

Nature's self-preservation instinct takes a strange twist in the Scandinavian countries. When food runs short, the lemming, an Arctic rodent, embarks on a death march to the sea, with only the strong surviving.

The short-tailed Lapland lemmings are extremely prolific and their numbers soon become too great to subsist in the mountains. Every five to ten years the entire lemming population starts a mass migration to the lowlands in search of food.

No obstacle stops their unswerving progress as they strip the earth of all vegetation. They swim lakes and streams, climbing over boats in their path, and most continue on to inevitable destruction in the sea. The few that are left return to the hills and start a new generation.

CAT EYES AND ELEPHANT BRAINS

The statement, "An elephant never forgets" and the question, "Why do cats' eyes shine at night?" are familiar to most of us.

Well the truth is that elephants do forget. If circus elephants are not rehearsed constantly they often seem very confused and uncertain. They forget all but the simplest tricks.

As for cats, their eyes shine at night because of light reflected by the tapetum, a layer of cells forming a large part of the inner eye. The tapetum is pink, gold, blue, or green and reflects a different color as the light changes. At night, the iris, or colored circle around the pupil, opens wider than it does in the eyes of man or other animals. The wide open iris lets in all possible light.

BRANDING AND CUTTING

Pictures in Egyptian tombs show that branding was practiced two thousand years before Christ. In the early days brands were made with a long piece of iron with a rounded point used to draw the brand on the animal's skin—called a "running iron." Stamping irons with the brand already made came next.

Today brands are kept on file in registry books at county courthouses. Brands consist of numbers, pictures and initials. They are a kind of code, read from left to right and from top to bottom. For example, a short horizontal line is a bar, a vertical line slanted to the left or right is a slash and a letter on its side is called "lazy." A box, diamond and circle are common designs. Earmarks are also used to identify cattle. They are used in addition to branding and are also registered. The ear is cut to mark it with a notch, split, fork, or some other pattern and they are easily identifiable in an ear because the cattle lift their ears toward an approaching cowboy.

THOROUGHBREDS

Watching a horse race has lured many people from their normal way of life in the past, but one of the most unusual occurred in 1877 when both Houses of the Congress of the United States moved to adjourn to view a three-way match race between Parole, Ten Broeck and Rom Ochiltree. Parole won easily.

Perhaps the fame of the horse alone is enough to enchant people. In 1932, Phar Lap, Australia's prize race horse, began his American career. Since the time someone had attempted to shoot him, two years before, he had been guarded day and night by five attendants and they had stayed with him constantly during his trip and after his arrival in this country. Despite this, Phar Lap died of colic. To satisfy the many American racing fans who had hoped to see the Thoroughbred, his mounted body was exhibited on a truck at a number of U. S. tracks and received tremendous ovations.

GREYHOUNDS REPORT CARDS

Greyhound racing originated in the United States, then spread to the British Isles, Europe, Australia and other parts of the world. Most United States tracks subscribe to the "grading system," which moves dogs to a higher grade when they win and to a lower grade when they fail for a given number of times to earn prize money. This tends to even the competition in every race. The grade of the race is indicated in the track program and racing forms have a barometer of each dog's ability.

The following is an example of how the grading system works from maiden up to grade AA. A greyhound is advanced one grade when in three consecutive starts it has earned six points in its current grade. A win earns six points, a place earns three points and a show earns one point. An exception is that maiden pups, upon winning their maiden race, automatically enter grade D instead of grade E. Grade A and B greyhounds are lowered one classification when they fail to finish first, second or third in three consecutive starts, fail to earn better than one third in four consecutive starts or are unable to accumulate the equivalent of a win purse in six consecutive starts. With slight variation similar conditions govern the status of a greyhound after it has attained grade AA status. Grade C and D greyhounds are lowered one grade if they fail to finish in the money in four consecutive starts.

LET'S HEAR IT FOR THE FOX!

Fox hunting was the last quarry to become popular in England. Until the middle of the eighteenth century the fox was barely considered worth the huntsman's attention. Before that a gentleman pursued the wild boar, the otter, deer or hare. They were usually trapped or shot as pests. The change came after the Restoration, when poaching had reduced the number of deer. From about 1750 onwards the sport of fox hunting grew until it became a part of English life. The strain of the foxhound was studied and improved. Horses were successfully bred for hunting. The traditional center of fox hunting is "The Shires," roughly speaking Leicestershire, Northamptonshire and Rutlandshire. Packs were spread all over England, however. Sometimes tenant farmers, local parsons or doctors rode with the packs. But mainly only the wealthy could find the time, maintain a stable and pay a hunt subscription.

IT'S ALL BULL

Bull breeding is a big business in Mexico because at least six of the animals fall to the blade in every sizeable city in the country every Sunday. Fighting bulls are taken from their mothers at six months. For the first two years they live a life of almost complete isolation. They are fed well but have no contact with men on foot, but only with bull tenders mounted on trained horses which seem to know by instinct when a bull is ready to charge. In a bull's second year—two years before he is to be fought—he is rounded up for a *tienta,* a test to see if he has the courage and fighting style for the ring. In these *tientas*—staged in private bull rings—there is nothing in sight for the bull but a man on horseback wielding a stick with a metal point. The number of times the bull charges and recharges the horse and the way he does it is noted carefully and placed in his record. The occasional "Ferdinand," wholly disinclined to fight, promptly becomes beef while his braver cousins go on to a more dramatic death. Bulls earn an "X" on their records if they show the qualities needed in the ring. This "X" signifies a *toro de bandera*—a flag bull. Such bulls bring several thousand dollars in a sales ring, but may go much higher in order to insure a successful Sunday show.

STATISTICAL OVERLOAD

Among Thoroughbreds a horse is a male animal five years old or more. Through his fourth year he is called a colt. The female of the species is a filly until the age of five when she becomes a mare and when she becomes a mother she is termed a broodmare. The father of a thoroughbred is the sire and his mother a dam. The dam's offspring is referred to collectively as her produce. The collective offspring of a stallion is known as his get. Prior to his first birthday, which is established as January 1 of each year, in order to avoid confusion, a Thoroughbred is known as a foal. When, in the fall of his first year, he is separated from his mother he is a weanling. After his first New Year's Day he is a yearling, and on the following January 1 he becomes a two-year-old and eligible to race.

Horses traceable to a common paternal ancestor are said to be from a particular line. Some 80 percent of all today's Thoroughbreds are traceable to Eclipse, foaled in 1764 and a great-great-grandson of the Darley Arabian. Matchem, foaled in 1748, a grandson of the Godolphin Arabian, accounts for about 15 percent while the remainder are traceable to Herod, a great-great-grandson of the Byerly Turk, and foaled in 1758. About 90 percent of registered Thoroughbreds are bay, brown or chestnut in color. The remainder are classified as grey, roan or black. A rare color is dun and white.

FOOD AND PLANTS

CORTEZ AND CHOCOLATE

Long before the discovery of America cacao was cultivated as a food by the Aztecs. When Christopher Columbus reached the New World, he learned of cacao and took a few beans back to Spain as curios, though he knew nothing of their food value. A few years later in 1528 when Cortez of Spain invaded Mexico, the real value of cacao was discovered. The importance of cacao beans to the Aztecs may be judged by the fact that they were used as a means of exchange or currency. When Cortez returned to Spain, he brought back news of a drink that was entirely unknown in Europe. The drink was called *chocolatl* and was in common use among the Aztecs. The term "cocoa" is derived from cacao and is universally used in English-speaking countries to designate the seed of the cacao tree.

When Cortez first entered Mexico, the emperor Montezuma entertained him and his followers at a banquet at which the only beverage was chocolate flavored with vanilla and other spices, whipped to a froth, and served cold. Montezuma drank no other beverage; it was served to him in golden goblets and after each one was drained, it was thrown into the lake that surrounded the palace. At one feast he emptied 50 goblets, while his guards and attendants consumed 2,000 jarfuls.

After Cortez introduced cocoa into Spain, it soon became very popular, although the Spaniards endeavored to keep its preparation a secret. In 1606 it became known in Italy, from whence it spread to Austria and was introduced in France by Anne upon her marriage to Louis XIII.

Chocolate houses became popular in both England and Germany in the middle of the 17th century. Spain controlled the world source of cacao and gained great wealth from its sale. So high a price was maintained that the beverage was beyond the reach of any but the most wealthy.

TEA AND HISTORY

The story of tea goes back so far that its true beginning is lost in time. Life was very simple and man had only a glimmering of his present-day knowledge when the Chinese Emporer Shen Nung knelt before a fire to boil water. Called the Divine Healer, the wise emperor always boiled water before drinking it. Nobody knew the causes of illnesses, but Shen Nung had observed that people who boiled their drinking water had better health. Shen Nung's servants made the fire from the branches of a nearby tree. As the water began to boil merrily, some of the topmost leaves of the branches fell into the boiling pot. "What a delightful aroma!" exclaimed the emperor as the fragrance of tea floated on the air for the first time. He sipped the steaming liquid. "Ah! And what a flavor!" That, the Chinese will tell you, is how tea was discovered around 2737 B.C.

The people of India have another story about the origin of tea as a drink. Some 1,000 years ago a saintly Buddhist priest named Darma wanted to prove is faith. He decided to do so by spending seven years without sleep, thinking only of Buddha. For five years Darma thought of Buddha day and night. Then, to his dismay, he found himself falling asleep. Darma fought to keep his eyes open. In desperation he snatched a handful of leaves from a nearby bush and chewed them, hoping that they would keep him awake. The leaves, of course, were the leaves of the tea bush. Darma felt refreshed and awake after chewing them. With their help he was able to complete his seven years of meditation without once falling asleep.

MUSTARD, KETCHUP OR BOTH

The first hot dogs are said to have been made by a butcher in Frankfurt, Germany in 1852. Tradition says that he shaped them like his dog, a dachshund. At about the same time a Viennese developed a similar sausage that was named wienerwurst, or Vienna sausage. In the United States the first franks were sold at Coney Island in 1871 by Charles Feltmann, a butcher from Frankfurt. Feltmann's name is almost forgotten, but one of his employees, Nathan Handwerker, established a Coney Island hot dog stand that is still a famous hangout.

Although Feltmann introduced hot dogs in the United States and Handwerker helped popularize them, two expositions in 1893 and 1904, respectively, in different cities – Chicago and St. Louis – claimed to have spread their fame nationally.

But it took a cartoonist, Tad Dorgan, to change the name to hot dog. He supposedly invented the nickname because he couldn't spell dachshund, the word used by vendors at football games at the New York Polo Grounds in 1900.

POISON ON THE PROPERTY

Do you realize that in your garden you could easily be growing poisonous plants? Who would guess that the beautiful oleander bush, grown indoors and outdoors all over the country, contains a deadly heart stimulant? So powerful is the toxin that a single leaf can kill a child. Some people have died merely from eating steaks that had been speared on oleander twigs and toasted over a fire.

The berries of the mistletoe have proved deadly to adults who used them to make a so-called medicinal tea.

Most dangerous of all plants in the vegetable garden is rhubarb. Its stalk, commonly used in baking and cooking, is not toxic but the leaf blade contains oxalic acid which crystallizes in the kidneys, causing severe damage.

Bulb plants such the hyacinth, narcissus and daffodil may be fatal. Ask a gopher—he knows.

THE GLOBAL ADVENTURES OF ALFALFA

Alfalfa was probably planted in southwestern Asia long before recorded history. Historical records show that man has grown alfalfa for fodder longer than any other forage plant. The Persians took it to Greece when they invaded that country in 490 B.C. Historians believe that alfalfa was introduced from Greece into Italy about the 1st century A.D. and later spread into other parts of Europe. Spanish explorers brought alfalfa to South America during the early 1500s and European colonists introduced it to North America.

The first recorded attempt to grow alfalfa in the English colonies was made in 1736 in Georgia. The colonists also took the plant to other areas, but it did not become important in North America until about 1850 when seed was brought to California from Chile. The Chilean seed produced excellent crops in the California climate. Alfalfa production gradually spread as far east as the Mississippi River and north to Canada.

NOTHING TO SNEEZE AT

More pepper is consumed in the world than any other spice, the percentages being about 55 percent pepper to 45 percent for the rest of the spice list. Back in 1492 pepper was high on Columbus's list of objectives when he was searching for a new route to the Spice Islands but discovered the New World instead. When Magellan tried to encircle the world, all his ships were lost but one. The pepper on board the vessel that managed to reach home paid for all the lost craft and allowed for a profit besides.

Black and white pepper are both ground from the berry of the jungle-born black pepper vine, whose formal name is Piper Nigrum. It grows on the Malabar Coast of India, in Indonesia—especially Java and Sumatra—the Malay Archipelago, Thailand, and Cochin China. For black pepper, the berries, which grow in clusters on vines trained to climb like a grapevine, are picked while green, are dried and then cured. Black pepper is cured by spreading the unripe berries on mats in the sun or suspending them over slow burning fires until they turn dark brown or black. Later, the whole berry is ground for table use. For white pepper, the berry is picked after it is fully ripe and the other shell is removed by bruising or washing, or more generally by steeping in water and removing the shell by friction. The dried kernel which remains after the outer shell is removed is white pepper and can be ground.

In the Netherlands and France coarse powdered pepper is used to prevent damage by moths and other insects when storing carpets and fur coats. The pepper is sprinkled on the material in the same density as one dusts flowers and plants. In the tropics, pepper is sprinkled in floor cracks and holes to keep out insects.

SAY CHEESE

From the Greeks and Romans, about 1000 B.C., to the present time, a milk product, commonly called cheese, has been given more than 400 different names. The cow, sheep, goat, llama, reindeer, buffalo and zebu all have contributed to cheese production.

Gourmets buy natural cheese—that made from whole milk with nothing removed or added except the microorganisms that give special flavor. Pasteurized cheese is something else. The process removes most of the bacteria that are essential for successful ripening. Processed cheese is simply watered down natural cheese, blended with such things as skim milk, water, spices and such.

Start your cheese tasting adventure by deciding on a flavor and how you want to use it.

Bleu, Gorgonzola and Stilton are "blue mold" cheeses, piquant and spicy flavored. They are excellent for appetizers and desserts. If you have a dessert in mind, choose a mild and nutlike flavor such as Edam, Gouda or Gruyere. Edam cheese can add an extra dash of color to the dessert tray. This creamy, yellow, cannonball shaped cheese comes in a red wax coat. Camembert and Brie have a mild to pungent flavor and are quite soft inside a thin, edible crust. They are two of the more highly flavored desert cheeses. If you would like a different cheese to grate and use as a seasoning, try Sap Sago. This hard cheese is a native of Switzerland, is made of soured skimmed milk with additions of buttermilk and whey and is flavored with clover leaves. It is marketed as a small, light green cone.

PLEASE PASS THE SALT

Thousands of years ago the Egyptians enjoyed a profitable salt trade with their neighbors. Many of their trade routes are still in use. The Phoenicians not only valued salt highly as a food seasoning, but also it became for them a symbol of trust and friendship. Contracts were bound with salt and many of the familiar sayings about salt originated in this early period of man's history.

Rome paid her warriors partly with salt, made in the form of coins and called *salarium,* the Latin word from which our "salary" comes. The Arabs considered salt a sign of good fortune and often burned it for luck before a caravan started on its journey. In ancient England, salt often determined the order of seating at meals. A large vessel filled with salt was placed in the center of the table. The nobility were seated above the salt, others sat below. The American Indian valued salt highly and often traded his land for the "magic white sand."

EAT YOUR VEGETABLES

Very few new vegetables have been introduced in historic times, and in many cases, little improvement has been made on the products of the ancients. Lettuce never had been found wild. It is believed to have first been cultivated in India or Central Asia. Herodotus, Hippocrates and Aristotle mention it in references to Greek gardens. Celery is a biennial plant native to the marshlands of southern Europe, North Africa and southwestern Asia. It was long considered poisonous and was not eaten until modern times. Pumpkins and squashes were grown in America long before Europeans came on the scene.

Peas are the oldest known vegetable. They are believed to have originated in Ethiopia and spread over Europe and Asia. They were eaten and possibly cultivated in Europe during the Stone Age. Columbus planted them in the West Indies in 1493 and they spread rapidly among the Indians and became one of the chief crops of the Iroquois. The species from which cabbage is derived grows wild in North Africa and along the European shore of the Mediterranean. It has been cultivated for 4,000 years. The turnip is a native of western and central China. The radish is a native of China and India. It was cultivated by both the Greeks and the Egyptians. The parsnip, another Asiatic root crop, was first planted in Virginia in 1690.

Popcorn, of course, is peculiarly American. In early Spanish writings reference is made to an Aztec ritual in which ":one hour before dawn there sallied forth all these maidens crowned with garlands of maize, toasted and popped, the grains of which were like orange blossoms – and on their necks thick festoons of the same which passed under the left arm."

A TWISTED TALE

Just as painters create masterpieces, so did a 7th century monk of northern Italy. An ancient manuscript on display at the Vatican, records that this unidentified cleric used scraps of dough left over from the baking of bread and fashioned them into shapes to represent the arms of little children as they appeared when crossed in grayer. The monk called his imaginative tidbit *pretiola*, the Latin for "little reward," and offered it as a prize to children who studied their catechisms.

Ultimately, the *pretiola* found its way across the Alps into Austria and Germany where, in the process of common usage, the name was changed to bretzel or pretzel.

THE ARTS

MUSIC

GENIUS AT WORK

Mozart once went incognito to the opera in Marseilles to hear one of his works performed. In one passage, through an error of the copyist, the orchestra played "D" where Mozart had written "D sharp." The composer sprang to his feet shouting, "Play D sharp, will you; play D sharp, you wretches!" Orchestra and singers stopped their performance and the audience began to hiss Mozart and cry, "Put him out!" He was about to be ejected when he identified himself. Then those who had wanted to throw him out cried, "Mozart, Mozart!" and led him to the orchestra pit where he was compelled to direct the opera. This time the missing D sharp was played in its proper place.

At the close of the performance Mozart received an ovation and was escorted to his hotel by the audience.

FIRST RECORDS

It is hard to imagine today that the record-making industry with its boom since the early forties has a history of faltering starts, success, disaster, success and disaster. In 1877, Thomas A Edison gave the phonograph machine its first practical form. In 1888 Emile Berliner produced the flat-grooved disk, forerunner of what we use today. In 1897 he took the device to Eldridge R. Johnson of Camden, New Jersey, who had a little machine shop, and through the initiative of these men, the commercial possibilities of records was established. They called their enterprise the Victor Talking Machine Company, and their first year's business amounted to $500. No. 1 in the first Victor catalogue was a recitation by George Broderick of Eugene Field's "Departure." A song, "I Guess I'll Telegraph my Baby," was one of the first musical numbers. The first operatic recording was in 1903, when contralto Ada Crossley sang an aria by Giordano, "Gel Caro Mio Ben." The first band recording—"Stars and Stripes Forever"—was made in the same year by John Philip Sousa and his band. Alma Gluck's recording of "Carry Me Back to Old Virginny" in 1911 became the first record "best seller." The first successful symphonic record was made in 1917 by the Boston Symphony Orchestra, Dr. Karl Muck directing. On February 1, 1904, Enrico Caruso made his first recordings. He sang ten operatic numbers into the big horn used in those days to make records and was paid $4000 for the afternoon's work. A year later, at his second recording date, he was paid $1000 for each number.

ORIGINS

Beethoven called the work Opus 27, No. 2. However, when the critic Rellstab heard the piece he was reminded of moonlight on Lake Lucerne and dubbed it the "Moonlight Sonata," a name that displeased Beethoven but still helped to make it one of the most popular classical compositions in the world.

When the weather was fair and calm in Roman days, it was called serenus. By the time this term reached the Italian language as sereno, it meant "open air," and a serenata was a piece played in the "open air," an evening song. The French accepted this word as serenade.

The term nocturne was first used by the 19th century Irish pianist and composer John Field who wrote some tranquil bits for the piano under this title. Chopin took over the nocturne and made it more somber and hence more suitable to the name, which is from the Latin word nocturnes, or "of the night."

RHAPSODY OF AMERICA

George Gershwin's *Rhapsody in Blue* is perhaps the best loved and the most frequently performed American work in the symphonic field. It is typically Gershwin and it is typically American.

It all started one morning in January of 1924 when Ira Gershwin read in his morning newspaper that Paul Whiteman was to give a jazz concert at Aeolian Hall on February 12. The concert was designed as a final vindication of Whiteman's belief that jazz was important American music, to be played and listened to seriously. To prove his point his orchestra would play a jazz symphony by the young composer George Gershwin. When Ira Gershwin showed this story to his brother George, the composer hadn't even thought of writing a jazz symphony. But Whiteman begged Gershwin to help him out, saying the concert was costing him $6000 since he was giving away all the tickets.

Gershwin capitulated. On a train trip to Boston he heard the rhythm and structure of his rhapsody. Within a week he had composed a rough draft. He revised, polished and reworked. Time was running out. Whiteman needed to rehearse and it took some time for clarinetist Ross Gorman to find a reed and experiment enough to play that ascending glissando which makes up the mood of the Rhapsody. Gershwin kept revising up to the last minute.

The greats of the music world turned out: Rachmaninoff, Godowsky, Stokowski, Victor Herbert, Walter Damrosch, Jascha Heifetz, Mischa Elman, Fritz Kreisler, John Philip Sousa and every important music critic in New York. The climax was the next to the last number, Gershwin's *Rhapsody in Blue*. With the first wail of Gorman's clarinet, the audience sat up straight. This was something new and different. The rhapsody was a tremendous success and the rest is history.

LOVE WITH NO STRINGS

The most brilliant period of Nicolo Paganini's life was from 1814 to 1818. He was poor at that time and was largely occupied with gambling and falling in love. Together with an excellent guitar player named Lea, he would wander all night playing under the windows of their friends. When tired they would drop into the nearest inn for refreshment.

One evening a rich man begged the pair, together with a cellist named Zeffrini, to serenade his ladylove. They consented, but before beginning to play, Paganini quietly tied an open penknife to his right arm. Then they commenced. Soon the E string snapped. "That was owing to the damp air," said the violinist, and kept on playing on the other three strings. A few moments later the A broke and Paganini exclaimed, "Just see what the dampness is doing this evening!" Finally the D snapped and the love sick gentleman began to be fearful for the success of the serenade. But Paganini simply smiled and went on with the music with the same result on only one string that he had previously used on four strings.

THE NIGHTINGALE

More than a century ago an artist who received the then fabulous sum of $1,000 a night was brought to America by the master showman, P. T. Barnum. Jenny Lind, "The Swedish Nightingale," not only possessed beauty and charm, but a rich, brilliant and powerful soprano voice. Her singing had already won adulation from every great musician of her time. Barnum's friends thought he was mad, but he grossed $700,000 from her tour. When she sang in Washington, D.C., there was no hall large enough to accommodate her admirers. An auditorium, built especially for her concert, seated 3500 people. Barnum decided to sell tickets for her concerts at auction. The first ticket brought $225. A few days later in Providence, Rhode Island, the first ticket auctioned brought the unbelievable sum of $650.

A GOOD OFFENSE

It is not often that we find a great composer and a prominent critic and musical writer in the same person. But Hector Berlioz was a critic and liked to make fun of fellow critics. To prove their incompetence he wrote a work called, "The Flight into Egypt," and put it on a program as the work of one Pierre Ducre, who was stated to have lived in the seventeenth century. The composition was in the antique style of that day.

The critics gave glowing tribute to the valuable work Berlioz had unearthed and even offered historical details of the life of the composer. When the admiration was at its height, Berlioz stepped in, claimed the work as his own composition and showed that such a person as Ducre had existed only in his imagination. By then the critics could hardly withdraw their unanimous approval, so Berlioz had his work favorably criticized by those who had previously torn him to critical shreds.

PIANO PLAYING MADE EASY

The first complete pneumatic player piano seems to have been one called a Pianista, on which a French patent was granted to a Monsieur Fourneaux of Paris in 1863. It wasn't successful.

E. S. Votey devised a pedal operated cabinet type of piano playing machine—a Pianola—differing little from a number of others, for the Aeolian Company, which patented it in 1900. Three years later the Aeolian Company formed a new corporation, controlling the manufacture of thousands of pianos to which it hoped to attach its mechanical masterpiece. Other piano makers scrambled to get in the player business. Control of speed and shading was made more sensitive and responsive to hand levers.

An enormous quantity of music was punched out on rolls—the latest popular songs, dance music and the classics, with the words to be read on the roll as it unwound. With the spread of electricity, pedal pumping gave way to button pushing. The player piano habit grew furiously. In 1905, less than six percent of all American pianos were of the player type. Ten years later the proportion was more than one out of every four and by 1919, the players outnumbered the straight piano and constituted more than 53 percent of the total annual output.

CRITICAL ACCLAIM

When the opera composer Giuseppe Verdi was completing his *il Trovatore* he was visited by a friend, a music critic, according to an apocryphal account. Verdi played him several parts of the work and asked his opinion. The critic called the Anvil Chorus "trash." Other numbers drew similar treatment. Verdi was delighted. "My dear friend," he said, "I have been composing a popular opera. In it I resolved to please everybody save the great critics and classicists like you. Had I pleased them I should have pleased no one else. What you say assures me of success. In three months *Il Trovatore* will be sung, and roared, and whistled, and barrel-organed all over Italy." Verdi was proved right.

A CLASSICAL BUZZ

Many a composer has been indebted to some sound or tone in nature for a musical idea. A good composer will turn to account a suggestion from any source, however humble. Felix Mendelssohn took pleasure in acknowledging his debt to nature in these matters.

A friend of his relates how they were walking in the country one day. Soon they sat on the grass in the shade and continued to talk. Suddenly Mendelssohn seized his friend's arm and whispered, "Hush!" A moment later the composer told him that a large fly had just buzzed by and he wished to hear its sound die away in the distance.

Mendelssohn was at that time working on his overture to *A Midsummer Night's Dream.* After it was completed he showed his friend a certain descending bass modulation with the remark, "There, that's the fly that buzzed past us at Schonhausen."

I'D RATHER BE IN PHILADELPHIA

How does a symphony orchestra differ from a philharmonic orchestra? It doesn't. Philharmonic comes from the Greek philos, meaning fond of, and harmonia, meaning harmony. Symphony is from the Greek word symphonia, meaning agreement of sound. The terms are used synonymously when applied to musical ensembles. One or the other or a combination of both is used by musical associations.

From its first concert on November 16, 1900, the Philadelphia Orchestra has been one of the world's leading artistic institutions. Fritz Scheel became the first permanent conductor. Scheel and his successor, another German, Carl Pohlig, laid the firm foundations of a great orchestra. In its thirteenth season Leopold Stokowski was engaged as the third conductor. Eugene Ormandy became the fourth conductor in 1936.

The Philadelphia Orchestra is one of the world's most traveled symphonic organizations. It was the first orchestra to make recordings under its own name with its own conductor (1917). It was the first major orchestra to broadcast over a radio network for a commercial sponsor (1929). It was the first symphonic organization to be televised nationally (1948). And, it was the first to be featured in films (*The Big Broadcast of 1937).*

QUIRKS

Composers' whims are in a class with the celebrated temperaments of many opera performers.

Gluck wrote best when seated in the middle of a field. Beethoven composed during or after a brisk walk in the woods. Wagner thought he must be clothed in the costume of the age and place in which the composition's plot was laid. His family was barred from his study. He would see no mail. His meals were passed to him through a trapdoor. Mozart could compose beautiful music while playing billiards. Haydn required white, best quality paper. Rossini was most productive when "lined within with good sack wine." He and Paesiello both enjoyed composing while in bed. Sacchini wanted a pretty woman by his side with his pet cats playing around him.

THE MET

Only two prima donnas in the history of the old Metropolitan Opera House had their own dressing rooms—Geraldine Farrar and, later, Kirsten Flagstad. They both chose the same airless, little cubicle nearest the stage. Miss Farrar's farewell on April 22, 1922, was the signal for a demonstration unmatched in the old house before or since. The Gerry-flappers, as her fan club was known, pelted the stage with flowers, dropped banners from the dress circle, loosed balloons and live doves into the auditorium from the balcony, and created pandemonium. Outside the theater the throng packed Fortieth Street for an entire block as the Met's stagehands bore their idol, wearing a gold crown, on their shoulders to her open car.

Neither Caruso's first or last performance at the Met caused much stir. The great Neapolitan tenor was only 30 when he arrived at the Met for the opening night of the 1903-04 season. No one suspected that *La Juive,* on Christmas Eve, 1920, would be the last performance of his life. He had spat blood on the stage of the Brooklyn Academy of Music during a performance on December 11. He sang at the Metropolitan two nights later, was stricken on Christmas Day, and died the following August at the age of 48.

THE SHAVE AND QUARTET

Joseph Haydn was one of those people who shaved himself when in a foreign country. In London in 1787, he lodged in High Holborn, opposite Chancery Lane, where one morning Bland, a music publisher, found him in the act of shaving. "I would give my best quartet for a good razor," growled Haydn. Bland took him at his work, bolted to his room in the same house, grasped his finest cutter and presented it to the composer. True to his word Haydn went to the drawer, pulled out the manuscript of his latest quartet, and handed it over to Bland. That composition today enjoys the name *Rasiermesser* or *Razor* quartet.

BIG BAND VENUES

The decade from 1936 to 1945 was sometimes known as the great band era. It was a time to go dancing and you went where the bands were playing. You went to the Manhattan Room of the Hotel Pennsylvania in New York, or to the hotel's Café Rouge. You went to Castle Farms outside Cincinnati, or to the Walled Lake Casino in Michigan, or to the Trianon or the Aragon in Chicago, or to the Palomar or the Palladium in Los Angeles, or to Glen Island Casino on Long Island Sound, or to Frank Dailey's Meadowbrook in Cedar Grove, New Jersey.

Radio networks began their nightly round of broadcasts at 10 or 11 o'clock and for four hours you could hear a different every half hour, one after another at America's grest dance floors. It was also a time when the first notes of a theme song would identify the band. It might be the swing band style of Benny Goodman, or the staccato trumpets of Hal Kemp, or the shuffle rhythm of Jan Savitt, or the bubbles of Shep Field's Rhythm.

THE FATHERS OF IMPROVISATION

The improvisation of serious music has become a lost art in the concert hall, but it was once a welcome feature of the performances of master musicians. Beethoven, according to his biographers, had the power of improvising so beautifully that he brought tears to his audience. Another musical immortal, famous for his ability to extemporize at the organ, was Johann Sebastian Bach. His *Musical Offering* was based on an original improvisation for the entertainment of Frederick the Great. After the time of Franz Liszt and his fellow romantics, improvisation languished, at least as far as public performances were concerned. In recent years only jazz musicians have devoted much attention to extemporaneous performance.

THE HIT PARADE – PART I

Many of us consider a musical masterpiece to have always been accepted as such. Debussy faced critical insults long after he had achieved world fame. The critic Hanslick, upon hearing the Tchaikovsky violin concerto, said the piece "stinks." Richard Wagner was derided when his opera *Tannhauser* was premiered in Paris in 1861. The ballet *Le Sacre Du Printemps* with music by Igor Stravinsky and choreography by Vaslav Nijinsky was the target of rioters when first performed at the new Theatre Des Champs-Elysees in Paris on May 29, 1913.

Instrumentalists also have had their share of knocks. Ignace Jan Paderewski's Paris debut was successful, but he did not fare so well in London. George Bernard Shaw, who was a music critic at the time, remarked that his "tempo rubato goes beyond all reasonable limits."

Pablo Casals' debut in New York back at the turn of the century was a failure. One reviewer was irritated by the cellist's reserved manner. Another criticized him for not smiling. But it took Stravinsky to administer the final blow. He said that "Casals made Bach sound like Brahms."

The man who had more failures than any other composer was Handel. His *Nero* was a failure. So were his *Rodrigo, Rolomeo, Ezio, Atlanta, Arminio, Giustine, Berenice, Semele,* and *Israel in Egypt.*

The greatest failure of all was J. S. Bach. He was all but forgotten. Two of his sons were better composers, said the critics—that is until Felix Mendelssohn dug up his manuscripts and began playing his compositions again.

THE HIT PARADE—PART II

Critics versus Beethoven is an interesting case. The composer received plaudits but also more than his share of detracting notices. A brief look at Beethoven's press clippings reveals bitterly critical reviews for many of his now most famous works.

The Second Symphony: "A crass monster, a hideously writhing, wounded dragon that refuses to expire, and though bleeding in the finale, furiously beats about with its tail erect."—A Vienna newspaper.

The Third Symphony: "It contains much to admire but it is difficult to keep up admiration of his kind during three long quarters of an hour. . . . If this symphony is not abridged, it will soon fall into disuse."—*The Harmonican, London.*

The Ninth Symphony: "But is not worship paid this symphony mere fetishism? Is not the famous Scherzo insufferably long-winded? The Finale is to me, for the most part, dull and ugly. . . . Oh, the pages of stupid and hopelessly vulgar music! The unspeakable cheapness of the chief tune, Freude, Freude. Do you believe in the bottom of your heart that if this music has been written by John I. Tarbox, now living in Sandom, New Hampshire, any conductor here or in Europe could be persuaded to put it in rehearsal?"— Noted Boston Critic, Philip Hale.

LITERATURE

WHO GETS THE CREDIT?

Was Shakespeare written by Sir Francis Bacon, Christopher Marlow, the Earl of Oxford, Sir Walter Raleigh, or possibly, even by Queen Elizabeth herself? All these and many other candidates have been seriously proposed at one time or another.

The earliest and probably the best known substitute proposed was Sir Francis Bacon— lawyer, essayist and philosopher. An English rector, the Reverend James Wilmot, suggested in 1805 that Sir Francis had been the true author of the plays. Other writers added color to the inquiry by professing to find a hidden meaning in the Shakespearean writings which pointed to other authors. One of the first to attempt such an interpretation was an American, Miss Delia Bacon. She wrote at length on the hidden "historical key," without ever actually divulging what it was.

Another amateur cryptologist was an American lawyer, Ignatius Donnelly. He said "Being satisfied that there was a cipher in the plays, and that it probably had some connection with the paging of the Folio, I turned to page 53 of the *Histories* where the line occurs: 'I have a gammon of bacon and two razes of ginger.' I commenced and counted from the top of the column downward, word by word, counting only the spoken words, until I reached the word 'bacon', and I found it was the 371st word. I then divided that number, 371 by 53, the number of the page, and the quotient was seven…. This I regarded as extraordinary."

The efforts to separate Shakespeare from his writings are based primarily on the assumption that Shakespeare's education and general background were inadequate to permit the wealth of classical reference and special knowledge of the plays, to say nothing of their poetic qualities.

FIRE AND REVOLUTION

Thomas Carlyle performed one of the most astounding feats of memory in history. After having written about forty-five thousand words on the French Revolution—the result of five months of work—Carlyle destroyed his notes and turned his completed manuscript over to his friend, John Stuart Mill, to read. One evening Mill went to Carlyle's home in a terrible state of mind. Mill's housemaid had used the manuscript to kindle a fire. Resting for a few weeks after hearing of the tragedy, Carlyle's *French Revolution* is considered by many to be his best work.

MARK & HUCK

In August, 1876, Mark Twain wrote to his friend William Dean Howells. He said he had nearly half completed a new book for boys. "It is *Huck Finn's autobiography*. I like it only tolerably well, as far as I've got, and may possibly pigeonhole or burn the manuscript when it is done." Twain met Howells in 1869, when Howells was the assistant editor of the *Atlantic Monthly*. The two men hit it off from the start. In personality, they complemented each other. They were both Westerners. Neither had had much formal education. At an early age both had gone to work as printer's devils in a print shop, and both had settled in New England—Howells in Cambridge and Twain in Hartford. Their friendship is perhaps unparalleled in American literature for duration and intensity, having lasted until Twain's death in 1910, forty-one years after their meeting.

The relationship between these two famous writers is recorded in many letters that passed between them during these four decades. Since they were both humorists, the letters are filled with laughter, gentle and raucous, shallow and profound. There are also many serious moments and moments of grief. It was Howells who persuaded Twain that Tom Sawyer should be a boy's book instead of solely for adults. It was Howells who along with Twain's wife objected to profanity in some of Twain's manuscripts.

On July 20, 1883, a letter from Twain to Howells informed his friend that he hadn't piled up so many manuscripts in years as he had done since the family came back to the Elmira farm: "Why, it's like old times, to step straight into the study, damp from the breakfast table and sail right in and sail right on, the whole day long, without thought of running short of stuff or words." He went on to explain that he expected to complete a kind of companion to Tom Sawyer in a couple of months—one that he had been working on for several years. When this companion to Tom Sawyer was finished, the author sent Howells the proofs. Reading proofs was sheer boredom for Twain, but Howells was a good copyreader. And so, seven years after sending Howells the first letter about *Huck Finn's Autobiography,* Twain finished his great book and had it published.

THE OLD MAN AND HIS CHILDREN

At one time during the reign of Louis XIV, Charles Perrault had been considered a leading intellectual of France. Now, living in retirement in the country, he was a tired old man. He had helped design the Louvre, had been a brilliant debater and poet, and had been the King's spokesman in the Academie Francaise, the nation's elite society of learned men. The few friends who visited him learned that now Perrault's time was spent in listening to foolish tales told by peasants. He would listen and then write down what he had heard. Those bits of so-called nonsense he wrote were to win him a place among the immortals. For Perrault recorded for the first time the age old folk tales of the French peasants—the children's stories still told throughout the world today. A few of the more famous were "Bluebeard," "Puss in Boots," "Little Red Riding Hood," and "Cinderella."

WHAT IF?

Booth Tarkington tells the following story about his writing *Monsieur Beaucaire:* "When I started I couldn't sell a story anywhere. I sent them to every publisher in the world, I guess, and they always came back. I had a friend who seemed enormously successful to me, and he asked me to illustrate a story of his. I could do that, at any rate, and I was very much pleased. Well, the magazine to which he sold his story failed, and there I was left with these illustrations on my hands. So I sat down and wrote a story to fit my illustrations and sold it as *Monsieur Beaucaire.* Wasn't that luck?"

Edward Everett Hale got his idea for the story of *Man Without a Country* from reading Scott's *Life of Napoleon.* It occurred to him that if Napoleon had been confined on one British warship after another instead of being sent to Saint Helena, England would have been spared much criticism and the French would not have been able to turn Saint Helena into a shrine. Local color for the story was gained from the records of the navy and the proceedings in the trial of Aaron Burr.

Rudyard Kipling's *Recessional* was published through another set of circumstances. After writing the poem, Kipling considered it inadequate and threw it away. Mrs. Kipling rescued it from the waste basket and sent it to the London *Times.* It was published on the date of the celebration of Queen Victoria's Great Jubilee.

WHAT'S IN A NAME?

Authors have been using pseudonyms almost as far back as the ancient papyrus writers, and for a variety of reasons. One reason is that authorship is rated low on the scale of social acceptability. In time, however, the profession has risen in esteem. Few authors nowadays bother changing their names—except in the mystery field. Some "mainstream" writers adopt a pseudonym for their mysteries because they feel that the contrasting forms of writing should be clearly differentiated by this device.

For example, John Canaday, former art critic of the *New York Times,* has also written several mystery novels under the pseudonym Matthew Head. There is John Creasy, the English mystery novelist whose large productivity was issued under more than a half dozen different names, the most prominent being, in addition to Creasy, J. J. Marric, author of the "Gideon" Scotland Yard series, and Kyle Hunt. There is Erle Stanley Gardner, who wrote about the celebrated Perry Mason under his legal name and about Donald Cool and Bertha Lam under the pen name A. A. Fair.

Some women mystery writers felt that their books would sell better if they were not clearly identified as female and hence would use masculine or neutral names. Elizabeth Linington used two additional names—Dell Shannon and Lesley Egan—both difficult to identify as to gender.

LITERARY FOOTNOTES

To the reader of *Treasure Island, Hiawatha,* or *Around the World in Eighty Days,* the plot is rather obvious. There are interesting stories relating to these three tales.

Treasure Island was written and read a chapter at a time for the entertainment of Robert Louis Stevenson's stepson, Lloyd Osbourne, then a 12 year old school boy, to relieve the tedium of a rainy vacation. It grew out of a map the author had drawn and labeled Treasure Island.

The real Hiawatha of history is thought to have been a Mohawk Indian chief who founded the Iroquois Confederacy in New York State. Hiawatha's name and title were hereditary in the Tortoise clan of the Mohawk tribe. It is thought the first Hiawatha lived about 1570 in central New York. He was a social reformer, interested in ending war and promoting universal peace among the Indian tribes.

As for *Around the World in Eighty Days,* Nellie Bly was a reporter on the *New York World,* and in November 1889, she undertook to make a trip around the world for her paper to demonstrate the feasibility of the adventure recorded in Jules Verne's novel. She accomplished the feat in 72 days, 6 hours and 11 minutes. She used steamboats, railroad trains and horse drawn vehicles exclusively.

THE YOUNG IMMORTALS

A few months before John Keats died in his twenty-sixth year he wrote to the girl who caused him much misery and ecstasy. "If I should die I have left no immortal work behind me—nothing to make my friends proud of my memory—but I have lov'd the principle of beauty in all things, and if I had had time I would have made myself remember'd."

Much of the best work of Keats, Burns and Tennyson was written when they were twenty-four—the age at which Alexander Pope published "The Rape of the Lock," Byron the first canto of *Childe Harold,* Shelly's *Alastor* and Swinburne two poetical dramas. Pope wrote the *Pastorals* at sixteen and Byron was throwing off live verses and lampoons at eleven. Ten thousand lines of *Pauline* were completed by the time Browning was twenty; the four thousand lines of *Endymion* when Keats was twenty-three; Blake printed his *Poetical Sketches* at twenty-six.

MARY AND THE MAD SCIENTIST

Theophrastus Bombastus von Hohenheim, a Swiss physician who died in 1541, compiled a volume called *One Hundred and Fourteen Experiments and Cures,* under the pen name by which he became famous—Philippus Aureolus Paracelsus. The English translation of this book came into the hands of the wife of poet Percy Bysshe Shelley while she was staying at the Lerici castle on the Italian Riviera. Fascinated with Paracelsus, Mary Wollstonecraft Shelley studied his writings and, while at the castle, wrote much of the *Frankenstein* manuscript, which was published in 1818.

Today there is reason to believe that her fictitious Victor Frankenstein, the mad scientist who created a live "hideous phantasm" from pieces of human bodies, was patterned after Paracelsus. Centuries ahead of his time, Paracelsus was one of the first men to think that animal tissue, if properly processed, could replace dead human tissue or trigger the growth of new tissue in human beings. For many years he experimented without much success on cadavers bought from city morgues. His tests involved the injection of a highly concentrated distillate made of animal brain cells into the brain of a person recently deceased. Paracelsus reported that one night one of his corpses stirred, emitted a hoarse groan and twitched its arms and legs for fully a minute. This led him to declare that such attempts showed the possibility of resurrecting and synthesizing life itself.

AUTHOR, AUTHOR!

As city editor of the Virginia City *Nevada Enterprise,* Samuel Clemens first used the pseudonym Mark Twain, the call of the pilots when taking soundings, meaning two fathoms. *Life on the Mississippi* is the story of a cocky young pilot whose crew made him the butt of a practical joke. While navigating one of the deepest places on the river they gave false soundings. He was frightened into ordering the engineer to back the ship.

The leadsman cry "Mark three; Quarter-less-three; Half twain; Quarter twain; Mark twain" suggested the name.

The derivation of William S. Porter's pen name is somewhat dubious. One source states that Porter got his pen name from a guard at the penitentiary where he spent five years for embezzlement; another source says that O. Henry was the name of a French pharmacist whose articles Porter had seen in the *United States Pharmacopoeia* when he worked in the drug store of his uncle.

In a paper, "How I Came to be a Writer of Books," Cincinnatus Heine Miller explains the origin of his pen name. His first writing was a public letter in defense of Joaquin Murietta, the outlaw. A Sacramento newspaper identified him with the outlaw and the name Joaquin clung to him, hence Joaquin miller.

POEMS AND SONNETS

The only writings of Shakespeare that were published under his personal supervision were his two poems *Venus and Adonis* and *The Rape of Lucrece*. Unlike the playbooks that appeared in his lifetime, they were carefully printed with scarcely any errors of the press. The proofs must have been corrected by the author. These were the young poet's bid for fame. Each of them is dedicated, in carefully chosen language, to his patron, Henry Wriothesley, the third Earl of Southampton. They were certainly the most popular of his writings. Sixteen editions of *Venus and Adonis* and eight of *Lucrece* had been issued by 1640. But after that, until the 19th century, they were little regarded.

Nothing in Shakespeare's non-dramatic writing is ever likely to rival the reputation of the *Sonnets,* among the most beautiful as well as the most perplexing poems in the English language. Their publication in 1609 can hardly have been supervised by the author, for they were carelessly printed.

SONGS

UNFORGETABLE—PART I

Jimmy McHugh, the composer, and Dorothy Fields, the lyricist, had been engaged to write the music for Lew Leslie's *Blackbirds of 1928,* a musical revue. The score went well except that one spot, which was to be the high point of the show, remained empty. It should be a remembered hit song, but neither Jimmy nor Dorothy could dream up an idea. Days went by. One evening, after a frustrating day, they went walking down Fifth Avenue in New York City. As they approached Tiffany's, that famous shop of expensive jewelry, they noticed a young couple gazing into the show window. The couple looked very poor, yet they clasped hands, and the fond glances they exchanged, spoke of a deep love that did not need money. Jimmy and Dorothy slowed their steps and the girl gave a cry, "Oh! Look at that bracelet! Isn't it a dream?" The boy put his arm around her and hugged her. "Gee, honey," he said, "I'd sure like to get you something like that, but right now I can't give you nothin' but love." Jimmy and Dorothy stopped short, looked at each other and the same words rang in the ears of each: "I can't give you nothin' but love." They ran to a piano and an hour later they had completed the song they needed so desperately for the top spot of *The Blackbirds of 1928*" "I Can't Give You Anything but Love, Baby."

UNFORGETABLE—PART II

The American composer Thomas Westendorf wrote a famous Irish song in 1876 as a musical confirmation of a promise made to his wife, Kathleen, that he would take her back to visit her old home. Following the death of her little son, Kathy Westendorf had wasted away. When Tom mentioned a change of scene from Virginia to her old home, Kathy smiled for the first time in months. However, he found himself short of funds. Hence, as an unsuccessful young composer, he had to fabricate new stories of success. One night when sleep wouldn't come, a wistful melody kept running through his mind. He crept downstairs and scribbled several pages of notes. He mailed the manuscript to the Cincinnati publisher who had rejected his former efforts. He waited and prayed. Finally a reply came. With it was a check big enough to cover the trip. Young Tom Westendorf had written the unforgettable ballad: "I'll Take You Home Again, Kathleen."

THE SONG OF HISTORY

Singing is a natural form of self expression that appears to be universal. Up to the fourteenth and fifteenth centuries, not much is known of secular vocal music, for none of it was written. Troubadours' songs were recorded about that time and in the compositions of these wandering singers are the beginnings of song as we know it today. Adam de la Hale is one of the troubadours of whose works we know a little, and Oswald won Wolkenstein, the last of German's Minnesingers, left a number of songs that have been collected.

It was in the late sixteenth century that composers began to write for solo voices, usually to be accompanied by the lute. In France, songs had been published as early as 1571, but an Italian, Caccini, claimed to be the inventor of the vocal solo when he published a collection of songs for the voice or the lute in 1601. During this time when the madrigal, a choral work like a motet but secular in character, had been brought to its peak, attempts were made in Italy to use a series of madrigals along with acting and pantomime on the stage. But the choral works were poorly adaptable to drama. A group of Italian composers then initiated a type of musical composition that substituted passages by single voices accompanied by chords for the elaborate passages of the madrigal. This led to the first opera.

THE GIRL FRIEND

During World War II, Lili Marlene was the girl friend of both sides. As the most famous Nazi song of World War II, Lili Marlene was translated into 19 languages, from which 49 versions emerged. The melody came from "Serbian Infantry March," written by the Yugoslav composer Mirko Silic, who borrowed elements of the tune from a German student, Norbert Schultze. When the German high command took over Radio Belgrade, the only phonograph record not shattered was Silic's march. It was played repeatedly as background music for the Nazi announcers' repetitious messages of victory.

A cabaret singer from Hamburg liked the tune, slowed it down and sang it with a poem called Lili Marlene written by a Hans Leip. But who was Lili Marlene? Hans Leip said that while he was a soldier in Berlin in 1917 doing daily sentry duty, he became enamored of two German girls at the same time. One was called Marlene, a young nurse from a nearby military base. The other was Lili, the daughter of a wealthy real estate man. So he wrote three verses about the two girls he admired from afar, but he made them into one girl, whom he called Lili Marlene. His poem was published in a German newspaper in 1917 and reprinted in 1938.

THE SINGING BARBERS

S.P.E.B.S.Q.S.A. are the initials of a society that claims to be the largest singing organization in the world. Now with chapters all over America, the Society for the Preservation and Encouragement of Barbershop Quartet Singing in America, Inc. was born in 1938.

Barbershop harmony is a style of vocal harmony which is indigenous to America. It is characterized by full four part harmony—that is, with a four part chord for every melody note. The voices are tenor, lead, baritone and bass, with the lead usually carrying the melody and the tenor consistent above, singing higher harmonizing notes, the bass singing lower harmonizing notes and the baritone filling in the chord, either above or below the lead. The melody may occasionally be sung by the baritone or bass, but not by the tenor, except for an infrequent note or two. It is invariably sung a capella.

A NATIONAL TREASURE – PART I

In the summer of 1893, Katherine Lee Bates, a young teacher at Wellesley College in Massachusetts, decided to spend her vacation discovering America. The rolling farmland of Ohio, the fields and streams of Indiana, the tall corn of Iowa and the acres of waving wheat in Nebraska all impressed her. The climax of her vacation came when she reached the top of Pike's Peak in a chartered prairie wagon.

During the long bumpy ride down the mountain, the first line of a poem insistently ran through her mind. A few days later four stanzas were penciled in her notebook and almost forgotten.

Two years passed before Katherine Lee Bates came across the poem again and sent it to a church publication. Although the verses were instantly popular, it wasn't until 1904 that a revised version was set to the familiar music of Samuel A. Ward.

Today Americans everywhere sing the lovely and moving work as a result of that summer vacation—"America, the Beautiful."

A NATIONAL TREASURE—PART II

"The Marseillaise" was written during the French Revolution by a young officer named Claude Joseph Rouget de Lisle. When a company of 600 volunteers was leaving Strasbourg to join the army on April 24, 1792, the major of the city planned a banquet in its honor. He asked Rouget de Lisle to write a song for the occasion. Rouget de Lisle picked out the tune on his violin, and it aroused such enthusiasm that 400 more men joined the company before it marched off to war. France adopted the song as its national hymn in 1876.

SING FOR YOUR SUPPER

During the early years of the century, song writers made their money from sheet music sales alone. With the rise of ragtime and dance bands, sheet music sales dropped sharply, taking with them the income of composer and lyricist and publisher. Finally in 1913 George Maxwell (publisher), Raymond Hubbell (composer) and Nathan Burkan (lawyer) decided it was time to do what European countries had done much earlier: form a mutual protective society of composers, authors and publishers. The first step was to get the backing of all musicians. The trio decided it was essential to enlist Victor Herbert's interest. When he became convinced of the need for a protective society, Herbert took the lead. On a rainy October evening in 1913, nine men showed up for a meeting at Luchow's restaurant. They committed themselves to the formation of a society and four months later, at a meeting attended by 100, the American Society of Composers, Authors and Publishers was officially organized.

It took many lawsuits and much money to establish the principle that the copyright owners of a song were entitled to receive pay for every commercial performance. Finally ASCAP began to function as a nonprofit collection agency for its members.

Later a rival organization, Broadcast Music, Inc., was organized. Today ASCAP continues to do what it set out to do: collect for its members or their heirs their share of profits for the public performances of their works.

What's in a name? Tin Pan Alley is the popular name for the area in New York City near Times Square where publishers of popular songs have their offices. It received its name because of the many tinny pianos playing different songs at the same time in the area. As a general term, Tin Pan Alley refers to the business of writing and publishing popular songs.

THEATRE AND DANCE

THE SUPERSTITIOUS STAGE

Peacock feathers suit a peacock, but old time actors believed that in the theater they spelled disaster. Superstitions were once very prevalent on the stage.

Whistling in the dressing room was considered bad luck, leading to the early discharge of the whistler. The spell could be broken, however, if the whistler would go outside the room, walk around a chair three times and spit. It was also bad luck to put a hat on a bed or hang pictures on the dressing room door. If an actor forgot something on leaving his dressing room he would not go back to retrieve it; instead he had the object handed to him over the threshold. According to tradition, no actor should ever sit on a wheelchair unless he used it in the play. Some stage superstitions had their basis in religion. A triple mirror could not be used on the stage, and three candles should never be mounted in one candelabrum.

It was generally considered very lucky if a cat walked across the stage during rehearsals, but when the cat was ejected from the theater it had to be through a door opposite the one it entered. It was good luck to put on the left sock first and to powder with the left hand, as well as to enter the stage or leave the dressing room with the left foot forward. If an actor's shoes squeaked as he made an entrance, it was good luck for the entire run of the play. Some actors refused to utter the last line of a play during rehearsal. It was to be reserved and spoken aloud the first time on the opening night.

ARABESQUES AND ATTITUDES

In ballet there are five basic positions of the feet, arms and head. There are three principal positions of the hand. The head positions are: head erect, head inclined to one side, head turned to one side, head raised and head lowered. There are an infinite number of attitudes. The pose is derived from the famous statue of *Mercury* by Jean Bologne (1542-1608). Carlo Blasis was struck with admiration on seeing this beautiful statue, and when he undertook the role of Mercury in his ballet, *The Festival of Bacchus,* he introduced a pirouette that concluded with this pose. In general an attitude is a pose in which the body is supported on one leg while the other is raised with the knee bent. The raised knee should always be higher than the foot. Arabesques are poses that doubtless owe their inspiration to antique painting and sculpture. The name arabesque applied to the flowing ornament of Moorish invention is exactly suited to express those graceful lines that are their counterpart in the art of dancing. An arabesque is made by supporting the body on one leg, while the other leg is extended in a straight line at right angles to it. There are five principal arabesques.

As a rule, choreographers do not work with a written or diagrammatic plan. Recall is largely left to memory. But preservation of the art of dancing and the self-protection of choreographers depend on recording dance composition in such a way that it can be read. The idea of inscribing dance is an old one. Margaret of Austria and Jean d'Orleans published dance books in the 1400s. Beauchamps designated the five classic ballet positions. Ladies of the French court read choreographies of ball dances as they would read novels.

All kinds of codes are used in dance shorthand—word abbreviations, tract drawings, stick figures, musical staffs, mathematical forms and abstract symbols. However, codified, written or graphed, the systems require study and then application once they are learned. They also take time. A notator may need two hours to transcribe eight bars of music and movement.

TWO SIRS AND A DAME

Asked to recall his most memorable Shakespearean experience, Sir Laurence Olivier, replies: "Perhaps the right answer is *Richard III* at the New Theatre on the night of September 13, 1944. We had rehearsed the play during the height of the flying bomb period in a large room in the National Gallery. The air raid warnings and all clears mingled with the words of Shakespeare, and it seemed doubtful at one time that the New Theatre would still be standing to receive us. But by the time *Richard III* opened things had quieted down and only the occasional reverberating roar of a V2 marred the tranquility of the West End scene."

Dame Edith Evans puts it this way: "The part of Rosalind gave me a sense of ecstasy that I have never quite realized in any of the others. To put oneself back into the heart and the body of such a lovely girl was for me a particularly enriching experience, for when I played Rosalind my girlhood was some way behind. And I remember after some of the rehearsals I used to be so excited that I would run a great deal of the way home."

Sir Donald Wolfit recalls this occasion in 1945: "On the aft troop deck of the *S,S, Durham Castle,* sailing through the Mediterranean with German U-boats below us, I was playing a performance of *The Merchant of Venice* with my full company in badly fitted khaki uniforms under a hot afternoon sun to an assembled audience of 1200 men, of whom only a dozen or so had ever seen a play by Shakespeare in their lives. The hisses for my Shylock and the cheer that rang out over the waters as Bassanio chose the right casket and won Portia—that was something, too."

THE SAVVY SAVOY

After only six years of collaboration Gilbert and Sullivan had such a strong hold on the public that their manager was planning a theater all their own. The opera *Patience* that had opened at the Opera Comique on April 23, 1881, was in October transferred to the Savoy which henceforth, was to be the home of the Gilbert and Sullivan operettas. It was a unique theater. There had been no important improvement in lighting since gas was introduced on the English stage in 1817. In 1881, daylight was still indicated on the stage by the yellow flicker of ordinary gas jets. But on October 10, 1881, the Savoy was the first electrically lighted theater in England. Moreover, it was the most comfortable theater in London. The attendants were forbidden to accept gratuities; the customary handbills, retailed at sixpence each were dispensed with and artistic programs were distributed free. Real whiskey was sold at the theater bars. The queue system, or waiting in line, was introduced at the pit and gallery doors.

HISTORY

U. S. HISTORY

BIRTH OF A NATION

The Constitutional Convention was planned at the Annapolis Convention held in Annapolis, Md., in 1786. All of the 13 states were invited to send delegates to the convention, which was going to consider the prospect of revising the Articles of Confederation. The Philadelphia Convention, as it was originally called, was to convene on the 25th of May, 1787, with 55 delegates representing 12 states in attendance. Rhode Island refused to send any delegation for fear that a revision of the articles would remove its power to tax. The 12 other states certified 73 men to represent them, but only 55 of this number ever reached Philadelphia.

Among the 55 delegates were several men who had fought in the Revolutionary War, served in the congress under the articles, or had performed some other service to their country. The presence of men such as George Washington and Benjamin Franklin helped the meetings progress smoothly. James Madison had undertaken a detailed study of various types of government before the convention began and was perhaps the most fit of the delegates to draft a new government document.

Madison also kept a diary of the proceedings which went on behind closed doors, and his writings furnish us with most of our knowledge about those sessions. He wrote that of the 55 delegates, about 30 were present at a majority of the sessions, which lasted continuously for 16 weeks. As the meetings went on, it became obvious that the articles were too weak to be revised suitably, so the delegates began to develop a new constitution of their own. When the drafting of the new constitution was completed, there were certain things which were not acceptable to all; but for the good of the majority, the delegates signed the Constitution, hoping that these things might be improved.

Fifty-two men were present on Sept. 17, 1787, when it was signed. Of these, 39 signed the document and three, George Mason, Elbridge Gerry and Luther Martin, refused because they were opposed to a strong central government. The remaining 13 members of the original 55 were not present, mainly because of their opposition to the new central government created by the Constitution. Forty men signed the Constitution, but the signature of the secretary is not counted as a signature of approval. After the signing the next step was ratification by the states. The Constitution stated that it would become law when nine states ratified it. It was ratified by the required number of states within one year of its completion. Delaware, Pennsylvania and New Jersey all ratified it in December, 1787. New Hampshire, the ninth state, ratified it in June, 1788. The last of the four states of the 13 ratified it in the order of Virginia, New York, North Carolina and Rhode Island.

From this time on, the Constitution was the supreme law of the United States of America, and any state desiring to be admitted to the Union was required to recognize it as such.

FLAG EVOLUTION

The first flags adopted by our colonial forefathers were symbolic of their struggles with the wilderness of a new land. Beavers, pine trees, rattlesnakes, anchors and various life insignia with mottoes such as "Liberty," "Hope," or "Don't Tread on Me" were affixed to the different banners of colonial America. The first flag of the colonists to have any resemblance to the present Stars and Stripes was originally flown by the ships of the colonial fleet in the Delaware River in December, 1775. It consisted of 13 stripes, alternately red and white, representing the thirteen colonies, with a blue field in the upper left land corner bearing the crosses of St. George and St. Andrew, signifying union with the mother country. This Grand Union flag was sometimes referred to as the "Congress Colors."

In January, 1776, this Grand Union flag became the standard of the Continental Army. Some Americans still believe that Betsy Ross made the first flag, although historians dispute this story. Another disputed story is that the first Stars and Stripes displayed in the face of an armed enemy was at Fort Schuyler, on Aug. 3, 1777.

Continental Congress passed a resolution that established the Stars and Stripes on June 14, 1777, but did not specify the arrangement of the 13 stars on the blue union, except to say that they should represent a new constellation. Consequently, some flags had stars in a circle, some in rows, some scattered on the blue field without any apparent design.

When the "Star Spangled Banner" was first flown by the Continental Army, General Washington is reputed to have described its symbolism as follows: "We take the stars from heaven, the red from our mother country, separating it by white stripes, thus showing that we have separated from her, and the white stripes shall go down to posterity representing liberty."

After the admission to the Union of the States of Kentucky and Vermont, a resolution was adopted in January, 1794, making the flag one of 15 stars and 15 stripes. However, Captain Samuel C. Reid, U.S.N., realizing that the flag would become unwieldy with a stripe for each new state, suggested to congress that the stripes remain 13 in number to represent the 13 colonies, and that a star be added to the blue field for each new state coming into the Union. This resulted in a law of April 4, 1818, that required that a star be added for each new state on the 4th of July after its admission but that the 13 stripes remain unchanged. There is no fixed order for numbering the stars in the flag, nor are stars assigned to particular states.

ONE VOTE SHORT

The year 1968 marked the 100th anniversary of the attempt to impeach President Andrew Johnson. President Johnson, a Democrat, had succeeded to the chief executive's position upon the assassination of Abraham Lincoln. He found himself embroiled in a running battle with the radical Republicans, who took issue with him on many points. Matters came to a head when the house passed a resolution impeaching the president on 11 charges. The hearing was held in the senate with Chief Justice Salmon P. Chase presiding. Thaddeus Stevens, long a foe of Johnson, was considered architect of the impeachment proceedings. Stevens was so ill that he had to be carried to the senate for the daily hearings. The hearing came to its climax on May 16, with a vote on the 11th article of impeachment. If it had been passed, it would have found the president guilty of high misdemeanor. The vote was tense. The outcome was 35 for impeachment and 19 against. Because it was one vote short of two thirds, the president was acquitted. The man who held the final vote—and who could have cast it against the president and so changed the entire outcome—was Senator Edmund G. Ross of Kansas, whose political career ended with that action.

President Johnson did not seek reelection and did not attend the inauguration of his successor, Ulysses S. Grant. Johnson returned to government as a senator from Tennessee in 1875, the only president ever to become a senator in later life.

JUMPING THE GUN

President Hayes was kept in suspense for four months as to the outcome of the election of 1876. This was one of the bitterest campaigns in history. Grant was the outgoing president, but his term of office expired on March 4, 1877, which was a Sunday. If Hayes were to be sworn in on Monday, March 5th, the country would be without a president for one day. Grant was worried. He gave an evening farewell dinner party on Saturday, March 3rd, to which Hayes and his wife were invited. Before the guests arrived for supper, Chief Justice Wait, and a small group, assembled in the Red Room where Hayes was quietly sworn into office. Announcement was not made to the guests at the dinner party, or to anyone else, until Monday.

In spite of the uncertainty as to who would be the new president, at least 30,000 visitors were in Washington to witness the inauguration. President Hayes was greeted enthusiastically.

The entire route of the parade was beautifully decorated. Ten thousand torch bearers marched up Pennsylvania Avenue, singing campaign songs. They crowded into the White House grounds and called for President Hayes. There was no inaugural ball, but a reception was held at the Willard Hotel.

FROM BILL TO LAW

What makes the United States a Federal Republic? We can tell by following a bill through the steps to becoming law.

Bills may be introduced by senators and congressmen on their own initiative; they may be recommended by the president to party leaders or to Congress; they may be framed by Congressional committees; or they may result from citizen proposals, lobbyists or special groups.

After a bill has been drafted in correct legal form, it may be introduced either in the Senate or in the House (except revenue bills, which always originate in the House). A bill is introduced in the House by placing it in a basket known as a hopper. It is read by the clerk, assigned a number and printed. The Speaker of the House refers it to the proper committee which may report favorably, amend, revise, rewrite or lay it on the table. In the latter case it is forgotten unless forced to the floor by a majority vote of House members or reintroduced in a succeeding session of Congress. If reported favorably the bill is put on the House Calendar. A second reading is given and it may be returned to committee. If the majority votes for the bill it comes up for final reading and, if it passes, is sent to the Senate. Similar procedure is followed in the Senate. If the Senate amends the bill the House must approve it again.

After the Speaker and Vice President sign the bill, it goes to the President for signature. At this point the President can sign the bill, veto it, or let it become law without his signature.

WASHINGTON'S STOCK

Today every student at Washington and Lee University can boast that George Washington still contributes several dollars a year to his education. How? In 1785, the General Assembly of the Commonwealth of Virginia awarded to General Washington a hundred shares of the old James River and Kanawha Canal Company in appreciation for his work on the project. Washington refused to accept the gift for his personal benefit, but agreed to take it if the Virginia legislature would let him turn it over to a public institution. He held the stock until it attained dividend value and then donated it, worth $50,000, to the Liberty Hall Academy, Lexington, Virginia. Since this was a large sum of money in those days—the largest ever given to an educational institution—the academy changed its name to Washington College. It later became Washington and Lee University. To this day the principal sum has never been touched. Only the interest, amounting to several hundred thousand dollars has been used.

Massachusetts issued paper money to pay its troops in 1690. This was the earliest issue of paper money in the American colonies.

In 1775, the Second Continental Congress issued paper money. This was the first national paper money issued jointly by the thirteen colonies. Paul Revere engraved the bills. So much Continental currency was issued that it dropped greatly in value. People came to say of any worthless thing, "It's not worth a Continental."

Prior to the Civil War, notes were the only paper currency issued by banks operating under federal or state charters. There was no federal paper currency. Treasury notes were the first paper money issued by the U. S. government itself, authorized under the acts passed in 1861 and 1862.

STATE BIRTHS

The United States experienced its last great surge of state making during the latter part of the nineteenth century. Only 14,000 people lived in the entire Dakota Territory in 1870. By 1885, there were about 550,000. In 1888 Montana Territory had nearly 140,000; Washington about 350,000, and Wyoming about 60,000. Nevada had fewer than 50,000 residents in 1888, yet had been a state since 1864. Because the other areas were Republican, the Democrats who controlled at least one house of Congress refused to admit any of them to statehood. When the Republicans finally won control of both houses of Congress they rapidly admitted all to statehood and even divided the Dakota Territory in two to increase their strength of the Senate.

Oklahoma was admitted to statehood after Indian land titles had been purchased. Before this, white settlers had to be ejected by troops since they were barred from this Indian Territory by Federal law.

Arizona and New Mexico became states in 1912, after their citizens had earlier rejected a Congressional offer to admit them as a single state.

DRIVING BY THE MAP

How did the custom of driving on the right side of the road originate? When were road maps first published in the United States?

The men who drove the Conestoga wagons along the early roads started the American custom of driving to the right. Americans had at first followed the English custom of driving on the left. The Conestoga wagon driver, however, either walked at the left of his wagon, sat astride the rear left wheel horse, or rode the "lazy board," a sliding oak board between the left wheels from which the driver could guide the horse and operate the brake. For the driver to have a clear view of the road it was necessary to keep the wagon to the right. Soon other vehicles adopted the practice.

Some road maps were published by bicycling clubs in the 1880's. But as a rule early motorists had to depend on written instructions form their automobile clubs. Road maps were first published in large quantities for sale to the public about 1910. William B. Akin, a Pittsburgh advertising man, is generally credited with developing the idea of the free road map in 1914. As a result of his idea, an oil company distributed many free road maps the following year.

THE MASON AND DIXON LINE

In the 1760s, two English surveyors and mathematicians verified the location of the disputed boundary between Maryland and Pennsylvania. It became the northern boundary of Maryland, Delaware and a part of Virginia which later became West Virginia. They determined the latitude of the line at 39 degrees 43 minutes 17.6 seconds—15 miles south of Philadelphia. A resurvey 130 years later, with modern instruments and methods, found the line at the northeast corner of Maryland differed by only 180 feet.

After having run the line about 244 miles west of the Delaware River, Mason and Dixon were interrupted by Indians in 1767, which prevented them from completing their planned work. Later surveys showed, however, that they had already surveyed about 30 miles beyond the northwest corner of Maryland.

The original stones for 5-mile marks on this line were carved in England from oolitic limestone. Lord Baltimore's coat of arms was shown on the Maryland side and the Penn arms on the Pennsylvania side. Intermediate milestones were smaller and were marked "M" and "P" only, on opposite sides.

WORLD HISTORY

FROM DOC TO GOD

Imhotep, an Egyptian physician, is honored in medicine as the first physician known by name. He lived about 2700 B.C. and served as vizier (prime minister) to King Zoser of the third Egyptian dynasty. His fame became so great that after his death the Egyptians elevated him to the status of a god and worshipped him for his healing powers. The Greeks identified him with their own god of healing, Aesculapius. Temples were built to Imhotep, and bronze statuettes of him have been preserved. A statue of him stands in the Hall of Immortals in the International College of Surgeons in Chicago.

Physicians have been putting their prescriptions in written form for more than 4,000 years. The oldest known medical prescription is a clay tablet marked with cuneiform script. It came from Nippur, a city in the ancient kingdom of Sumer, which covered the southern portion of present day Iraq. Physicians were among the first persons to write on clay.

THE OLD FLORENCE DRUG STORE

The oldest practicing pharmacy in the world is open to every tourist in Florence, Italy. Opened in 1612 by monks, the Officina Profumo Farmaceutica di Santa Maria Novella di Firenze is a drug store without peer anywhere in the world. Marta Stefani Bernardini, whose family has owned the pharmacy for nearly a century, explains that all of the products are originals and are not distributed by companies. The medicines, perfumes, liqueurs and cosmetics are concocted according to formulas worked out by monks in the 17th century. Liqueurs include sweet elixir of rhubarb and sweet elixir of cinchona. Cosmetics include rice powder and iris flower soap and sachet.

Some of the big sellers are scents, which are always called essences because they are not perfumes. Among those sold are triple and quadruple essences for handkerchiefs and essences that evaporate quickly. Some of these are used by customers to heighten desserts. On the shelves is one of the world's oldest medicines—Teriaca, which began with Mithridates who died 63 years before Christ. Originally Teriaca was made from Balsam fruit, myrrh, nard, Cretan dittany, Celtic spikenard, Jewish bitumen, earth from Lemnos and balm of Gilead. Today Teriaca is made of nutmeg, butter, hyssop, Imperico, clarified butter, Gentian root, Comedrios and Ivatetica. During the Middle Ages Teriaca was prescribed for everything from bubonic plague to ingrown toenails. The Florence pharmacy makes up a supply every 30 years since now there is little demand for it. If you wish to buy some at $16 a smidgen and taste it, it will remind you of quinine.

DEAD SPELUNKING

If the Catacombs near Rome were placed in a straight line, it is estimated they would extend for more than 600 miles. Their total area is about 700 acres. Cut out of the soft tufa in the hills surrounding the city, they ceased to be used as a burial place after Alaric's sack of Rome in A.D. 410.

During the Middle Ages, their sites seem to have been almost forgotten, but interest was revived by the scientific discoveries of a Maltese, Antonio Bosio, known as "The Columbus of the Catacombs." The galleries and subterranean chambers are built layer below layer and are so intricate it is easy to lose one's way.

THE BRITS

The British Commonwealth of Nations covers about a quarter of the entire land surface of the earth. How did such a vast commonwealth start?

The mistakes that caused the breakaway of the Thirteen Colonies might have been repeated in Canada. In the eighteenth century, Canada was divided into Upper Canada (Ontario) and Lower Canada (Quebec). Each province had its own representative government, but the full executive powers were still kept by Britain. Both the British and French populations in Canada remained loyal to the British cause during the last period of the Napoleonic Wars in Europe. In 1837, however, independent uprisings took place in the two provinces. Fortunately, the British Government realized its responsibility and John George Lambton, the first Earl of Durham, was sent to investigate. His report, one of the most important documents in colonial history, said that the only way of securing harmony was to give Canada a government that possessed full responsibility for the public affairs of the country.

This immense step forward was taken despite political predictions that it would lead to the dissolution of the British Empire. In effect, however, the simple recommendation of the Durham Report is the charter of the British Commonwealth.

WARS AND BATTLES

THE 500 PLUS YEAR TREATY

Many treaties are just as famous now as they were centuries ago. Some are remembered only by a handful. One such treaty made between King Ferdinand of Portugal and Great Britain in 1386 was of the latter kind. The Treaty of Windsor provided that each party would assist the other in case of war or invasion. When World War I broke out the ancient alliance was brought to light and Portugal committed herself to the aid of the British. She thereby entered the war by virtue of a 6528 year old treaty which only one person in thousands of either country had ever heard of. Minor hostilities took place between Portugal and Germany in the summer of 1914. Britain had not encouraged any unnecessary intervention by Portugal, but agreed to her requisitioning 36 German and Austrian ships interned in Portuguese harbors. Germany retaliated by declaring war on March 9, 1916. Portuguese troops fought side by side with the British and Belgians in the African campaign and on the Western Front, thereby honoring a treaty over five centuries old.

WHAT'S IN A NAME?

Waging war is common to man, ants, termites, and bees. Primary considerations to each are property rights and self-preservation. Not so common in many cases have been the names applied to wars. For example, the first seven North American wars after colonization were identified one way in the New World and another in the Old.

Three of these conflicts, fought between 1689 and 1748, have come down in European history as the War of the Second Coalition against Louis XIV, War of Spanish Succession and War of Austrian Succession. Their New World counterparts were known as King William's War, Queen Anne's War and King George's War.

Subsequent wars in Europe, from 1756 to 1815, took the names of the Seven Year's War, War of American Revolution, French Revolutionary Wars and Napoleonic Wars. But on this side of the Atlantic, history records them as the French and Indian War, American Revolutionary War, Undeclared French War and the War of 1812

THE LUCK OF CORTEZ

In Mexican mythology Quetzalccoatl was half god and half man. He was revered as having brought mankind into being by a gift of his own blood. Traditions in the form of mythological tales predicted the return of Quetzalcoatl in the year that Europeans count as 1519. It so happened that on Good Friday of that year, Hernando Cortez landed at the sight of modern Vera Cruz. He had only 508 soldiers under his command and faced a native army estimated to have numbered at least 48,000. When the opposing forces met in the Battle of Cintla on March 25, it was 16 horses that turned the tide. Never having seen a human being riding an animal, native warriors thought horse and rider to be one. To compound the dilemma, most of the Spanish fighting men wore long beards of the sort associated with the hero god whose imminent return was anticipated. There was but one conclusion and that was that Quetzalcoatl had returned. The Mexicans knew they couldn't defeat the forces of their own god man, though they outnumbered them by a ratio of about one hundred to one. They retreated from Cintla in confusion and Cortez was on the way to mastery of a continent with a handful of men.

THE FIFTH COLUMN

The Spanish Civil War of 1936-1939 gave us the expression "fifth column." General Emilio Mola, in command of the Nationalist troops marching against Madrid, remarked, "We have four columns on the march outside the city. In the city we have a fifth column."

He was referring to people working for the Nationalists within the city. Although he considered them part of his army, the fifth column was physically separated or "out of place." The term has since come to apply to nationals of any country working for the enemy.

OF TRAINS AND SHIPS

In April, 1862, a Union spy named James J. Andrews led 21 men through the Confederate lines to Marietta, GA., where they captured the railroad engine, the *General*. They ran it northward toward Chattanooga, Tenn., destroying telegraph communications as they went. But Confederate troops in another engine, the *Texas,* pursued the *General* and caught it after an exciting chase. The confederacy hanged Andrews and seven of his men.

Almost three years later the Civil War was still raging. But on Feb. 3, 1865, representatives of the North and the South met on board the ship River Queen in Chesapeake Bay. The ship was anchored at Hampton Roads, near Fort Monroe. President Abraham Lincoln and Secretary of State W. H. Seward represented the North. The Confederacy's vice president, Alexander H. Stephens, Senator Robert M. T. Hunter and Assistant Secretary of War John A. Campbell represented the South.

President Lincoln refused to change any terms of the Emancipation Proclamation or consider any peace proposal that did not involve immediate restoration of the Union and the laying down of Confederate arms. The Hampton Roads Conference failed to end the Civil War.

HUMAN DEVELOPMENT

HUMAN FEATS AND CREATIONS

CATCH ME IF YOU CAN?

What was the longest run made in a football game? A quick review reveals one standard that according to today's rules will never be beaten—officially. Yale's Wyllys Terry in the Wesleyan game, November 4, 1884, grabbed a pass from center while standing in punt formation, five yards behind his own goal line, ran the entire length of the then 110 yard gridiron, a distance of ll5 yards in all.

But what about the longest lope ever made in a football game? The record books don't specifically say so but probably one of the longest was made in a contest between two semi-pro teams in 1939, the Ironwood Polar Bears of Ironwood, Michigan and a team from Minneapolis. The Polar Bears' backfield man, Harry Newby, receives the ball on his own 27 yard stripe, around 10 yards from the right sideline. Harry slants off tackle, bearing left toward the opposite side, in an oblique direction, and gets as far as his 39 yard marker where a group of rival players force him to turn backward, in the direction of the far side line when he's compelled to retreat a second time over almost the identical space that he has traveled, back to his 16 yard marker. Once more he circles toward his left and the right side of the field and advances now to the 25 yard line. There, for the third time, he is forced back toward his own goal line. About 18 yards in from the right side line and 16 yards from the Polar Bears' own goal, he heads right again, and turning in a short arc 5 yards from the edge of the field, heads for the rival goal. By now the opposition is so beat that Harry has a clear field and legs it down the gridiron to the rival's 10. At the 10 yard line Newby cuts to his left and heads directly for the goal, where he completes the 265 yard lope—probably the longest in the history of football.

OF PAINTERS AND PAINTINGS

Mona Lisa, finished after the turn of the 16th century, was one of four paintings that the artist, Leonardo Da Vinci, took from Italy when he went to France under the patronage of King Francis I. When Da Vinci died, the king, by prior agreement, took possession of the Mona Lisa and hung it in the royal chateau in Fontainebleau. As state property, it passed from monarch to monarch.

When the Louvre was a royal palace it hung there. Louis XIV admired it so much he had it hung in his bedroom at Versailles. After the revolution the painting was moved back to the Louvre. Not to be outdone, Napoleon had it put in his room.

In 1911, Vinzenzo Peerugio, an Italian, stole the painting and returned it to Italy, he said, for patriotic reasons. Two years later the Louvre recovered it.

Rosa Bonheur, famous French animal painter (1822-99) gained knowledge of her subjects the hard way. In her back yard she kept a private zoo, consisting of lions, chamois, goats, deer, gazelles, monkeys and other animals. She put on male attire and visited the Parisian stockyards and slaughter houses to study animal anatomy first hand. Her ability to capture animal likenesses won her a reputation as the finest animal painter of her time, although the French emperor twice denied her the Legion of Honor because she was a woman. Later, Empress Eugenie made amends by personally decorating her.

Blue Boy is one of the most important paintings by Thomas Gainsborough, the eminent English artist. This portrait was painted when he was at the height of his fame, reportedly to refute an argument of Sir Joshua Reynolds that blue was a color unsuitable for the main light of a work.

FINALLY!

The attempts to climb Mount Everest, the highest peak on earth, began in 1921. In all, there were eleven expeditions to the mountain before it was finally conquered. All but two of these were British and one of the most notable took place in 1924, when George Leigh-Mallory and Andrew Irvine struggled to within a thousand feet of the top, only to disappear forever. Then on May 29, 1953, victory was won by a British group under Col. John Hunt when Edmund P. Hillary of New Zealand and Tenzing Norgay, a Sherpa native, became the first men to reach this highest point on earth.

Later successful attempts include those by a Swiss team in May 1956, by the American James Whittaker and a Sherpa native on May 1, 1963, and by four Americans, who made a double conquest from opposite sides of the peak on May 22, 1963.Everest was finally climbed, scores of Himalayan peaks almost as high remained unscaled. Notable among them were Mount Godwin Austen or K2, the second highest mountain in the world and Kanchenjunga I, often considered the most formidable challenge of all. In 1954, Godwin Austen was conquered by an Italian expedition and in 1955, Kanchenjunga I was scaled by a British group.

MISS LIBERTY

The Statue of Liberty, symbolic gateway to America, offers a panoramic view of New York harbor. This greatest lady of them all hasn't lost her face or figure despite wind, rain and war.

She cost the French $700,000 to cast in 1886 and then had to mark time for almost ten years while the United States agreed upon a location and raised $300,000 for her installation. Boston, Philadelphia and New York all vied to be her home despite initial charges that such a statue was both pagan and idolatrous.

Miss Liberty, 152 feet tall and 35 feet around the waist, is built to withstand a gale up to 141 miles an hour. Her right arm is 47 feet long, her index finger 7 feet long, her head 10 feet thick, her nose 4 ½ feet long, her mouth 3 feet wide and each eye is 2 ½ feet wide. She has 7 spikes in her crown, 11 points in her star-shaped pedestal. She holds a torch in one hand and in the other a tablet on which is inscribed the date of the Declaration of Independence.

Liberty Island was chosen for Miss Liberty by the sculptor Bartholdi on his first visit to the United States. It was originally called Bedloe's Island after Isaac Bedloe, its first owner, who had a farm there. The island belongs to New York City but the waters around it are in New Jersey.

THE DIVER AND THE BOOKIES

Although high diving from either platforms or cliffs is dangerous, it is usually not done with the idea that the diver will get killed. This was not so when one of the highest dives on record was made in 1918 from a cliff near Melbourne, Australia, by Alexander Wickham, a native of the Solomon Islands and a champion swimmer. While on vacation there, Wickham accepted the proposal of a group of bookmakers to jump from a cliff 206 feet above the water, or as high as a seventeen story building. He had not seen the cliff and he did not know the height at the time he agreed to it. At first Wickham refused to keep his promise, fearing the dive would kill him, but he finally consented.

Many bets were made by the bookies, who offered odds of five to one that Wickham would not dare to dive, and ten to one that he would not survive if he did it. He finally made the leap and lived, although he was unconscious for hours afterward and his body was black and blue for months.

THE AMAZING SNOWSHOE

To John Thompson, a giant statured Norwegian born rancher in the Sacramento Valley of California, skiing became work and not sport. Late in 1856, Thompson learned that settlers on the eastern side of the Sierras were cut off from communications by heavy snow. From his early boyhood memories he fashioned oak wood "Norwegian snowshoes" that were 10 feet long and about 4 inches wide and weighed 25 pounds. After some practice with them, he strapped a sack of mail on his back and set out. He made the mountain crossing in three days, returned to his ranch, and was in business.

For twenty years thereafter, "Snowshoe" Thompson spent his winters skiing back and forth with pack loads of mail and merchandise that sometimes weighed 100 pounds, at a fee of 50 cents a pound. Much of the type that started an important Nevada newspaper went in on his back. When he died in 1876, at the age of 49, still going strong, his grave was honored with a headstone carved with a pair of "Norwegian snowshoes."

PROMONTORY

At about 12:45 p.m., on the afternoon of May 10, 1869, former Governor Leland Stanford of California, president of the Central Pacific Railroad Company, aimed the tap of a silver plated sledge at a ceremonial spike of Mother Lode gold, which had been inserted into a tie of polished California laurel he had brought to Promontory Summit, Territory of Utah, for the occasion. He swung and missed. Dr. Thomas Durant, vice-president of the Union Pacific Railroad, swung and missed also. Stanford swung another sledge, this time at a real railroad spike linked to the Western Union telegraph lines recently strung along the roadbed. As his sledge, which was similarly wired, tapped the spike, the impulses became dots heard in Sacramento, San Francisco, Chicago and New York simultaneously. They added up to a message of but one word: "Done!" The time was 12:45 p.m. The manual labor completed, a message was tapped out to President Ulysses S. Grant: "The last rail is laid, the last spike is driven. The Pacific Railroad is completed. The point of junction is 1,086 miles west of the Missouri River and 690 miles east of Sacramento City."

Behind those century old ceremonies, at the long gone shack town of Promontory, lay 300,000 tons of iron rails, 1,700,000 bolts, 6,000,000,000 ties, and 23,500,000,000 spikes.

A STRAIGHT STREET

Where would you see the "street called straight?" In Damascus, capital city of Syria. This ancient city is beautifully situated on a plain covered with gardens and orchards and watered by the Barrada. The charm of Damascus has often been ecstatically described by travelers. Many of its streets are narrow, crooked and dilapidated and, except in the wealthy Moslem quarter, the houses are low with flat arched doors.

But the "street called straight," mentioned in connection with the conversion of the Apostle Paul, is about 2 miles long and runs from northeast to southwest, almost through the center of the town. In the time of Paul it was a magnificent thoroughfare, 100 feet wide, flanked with Corinthian columns. Today it remains busy but is much narrower and less ornate.

GEORGE AND THE OBELISK

Did you know that the Washington Monument has two cornerstones; or that it was once stolen and held for three years; or that one stone from the Pope was dumped into the Potomac and never recovered?

The monument nearly took three other forms before it was decided to build it in the shape of an obelisk. It might have resembled a temple or a colonnade around a blunt topped shaft or a mausoleum in the proportions of a pyramid.

Eventually, the plan and site were chosen. The cornerstone was a huge piece of marble weighing more than 12 tons. A crowd of 15,000 to 20,000 people watched as Grand Master French of the Masonic Order wielded the same trowel used by George Washington in laying the cornerstone of the Capitol fifty-five years earlier.

The structure rose steadily for the next six years, reaching a height of more than 150 feet. The stone from the Pope, one of many donated by foreign heads of state, drew vehement protests from members of the Know-Nothing Party and was consigned by them to its watery Potomac grave. The party then gained control of the monument by breaking into the Washington National Monument Society's office, stealing records and books and electing its members the new officers.

In 1880, a second cornerstone was laid and construction of the shaft was resumed. A little more than four years later the great 3300 pound capstone was lowered into position. On its peak was placed the 100 ounce point of aluminum. The completed monument is about 555 feet high. At time of completion, it was the highest building ever erected.

THE TRAGIC STORY OF A BROKEN ROPE

Men and women climb mountains because mountains are there. One of the most famous and tragic climbs in history was Edward Whymper's ascent of the Matterhorn. At that time the mountain was considered invincible. In 1865, after trying several times without success to make it from the Italian side, Whymper gathered a group together at Zermatt to try it from the Swiss side. The party consisted of Whymper; Lord Francis Douglas, a practiced climber; Peter Taugwalder, a veteran guide; his son peter; the Reverend Charles Hudson, possibly the ablest English mountaineer of the day; Michel-Auguste Croz, the great guide from Chamonix; and Douglas Hadow. Hadow's inexperience, which was unknown to Whymper at the time, proved to be the cause of the tragedy.

The climbers reached the summit on the second day and after an hour started down. Croz had to turn around every few steps to place Hadow's feet in their proper positions. At one such moment the tragedy occurred. When Croz turned, Hadow lost his footing and fell against the guide. This in turn pulled Hudson and Douglas off balance. The two Taugwalders and Whymper grabbed at the nearest rocks but felt nothing after a terrific jerk of the rope. It had broken and the four mountaineers slide downward on their backs, spreading out their hands, hoping to save themselves. They dropped out of sight to the glacier below, a distance of almost 4000 feet. It was later discovered the rope had been their third best and was to be used only in case of an emergency.

A FEAT OF FEET

The Olympic Games were held in Berlin in 1936 and Adolph Hitler was confident his "master race" would demonstrate its superiority to the rest of the world. But Hitler failed to take an American black man, Jesse Owens, into account. Owens captured four gold medals—an unequaled feat to that time. In doing so, he broke three Olympic records and tied a fourth. The victories which won Owens fame as the greatest track star of the century, were in the 100 meter dash, broad jump, 200 meter dash and the 400 meter relay. As a leadoff man in the relay, Owens established a lead for his team which was never seriously threatened. After his performance, Owens was welcomed home by a ticker tape parade in New York at which one admirer tossed a brown paper bag containing $10,000 into his car. He discovered it hours later.

During his student days at Ohio State University, Owens stood out as an amazing athlete. On May 25, 1935, during a meet between Ohio State and Michigan, he set three world records and tied a fourth. One of those records, a broad jump of 26 feet 8 ¼ inches, went unbeaten for 25 years. Fifteen years after his Olympic feat, new honors came Owens's way when Big Ten track coaches and Associated Press sportswriters voted him the track athlete of the century.

THE DEVIL'S SLIDE

The record holding bobsledders of today take second place to a form of mountain sliding that occurred many years ago down New England's highest peak, Mount Washington. The 3 ¼ mile cog railway up this mountain climbs at a grade of 1 in 4. Its locomotives claw their way up on gears meshing with a wide rack rail laid between the regular irons. This incline made track walking difficult, so the workmen invented a unique piece of railroad equipment—a 3 foot by 1 foot slab of wood and metal grooved to fit over the greasy rack rail. This slide board became known as the Devil's Shingle. A workman would seat himself with knees drawn up, and then after easing off twin hand brakes that gripped the rail, could slide slowly down the track. Experienced riders soon were making the run, which had a drop of 3,700 feet from summit to base, in 3 minutes averaging 65 mph. The record time was 2 and ¾ minutes, close to 71 mph. When one man was killed and another seriously hurt, the Devil's Shingles were scrapped and further sliding forbidden.

THE BRIDGES OVER TIME—PART I

The basic designs used by modern bridge engineers have been around for centuries. The first masonry stone arches were built 6000 years ago in Egypt and Mesopotamia. Residents of Switzerland in 500 B.C. were among the first to derive timber piles into water to form piers for over water construction. The Tibetans apparently were the first to realize that suspension bridges could be built by hanging a framework of branches from vines stretched across a canyon. The ancient Chinese produced the first cantilevers with clumsy wooden beams.

There are five basic bridge designs although no two are exactly the same. The girder bridge is the simplest and often the most economical. It consists of a straight horizontal beam resting on a series of straight vertical supports. The truss bridge derives strength from a series of triangles and can support heavy loads over long distances. The arch bridge is one of the most beautiful styles because of its rainbow curve. The arch gets strength by pushing outward against heavy abutments built on shore. The suspension bridge is the most popular for long crossings. Three basic parts are the cables to carry the roadway, heavy anchorages on both shores to secure the ends of the cables, and towers to support them. The cantilever bridge was once very popular because of its rigidity, relative economy and ease of erection. In recent years, it has lost some of its popularity because of its apparent complexity. Steel cantilever arms are built outward from towers and the space between them is filled with a short suspended span.

THE BRIDGES OVER TIME—PART II

If you think New York City as well as Venice, Italy, had a Bridge of Sighs, you are right. In New York it was a covered passageway between the Tombs Prison and the former criminal courts building. It was built so that prisoners could be escorted from the prison to the court rooms without crossing the street.

The Venetian Bridge of Sighs, built by Antonio Contino in the 1500s, spans the canal between the Doge's Palace and the state prison. It received the name because of the unhappy prisoners who had to cross it. They went from the prison to the palace for trial through one passageway of the bridge. If found guilty, they were sent back to execution through another passageway.

CULTURE AND CUSTOMS

HOME SWEET HOME

The early North American Indians had no tables, chairs or stoves. Their only furnishings were beds, which were seats of matting covered with bearskin. These seats extended around the walls of the house and were about two feet from the ground, but the entire household often slept on the floor around the fire. They had no chests or cupboards. From poles near the top of the house hung clothing, weapons and skins, as well as meats, corn and other food. The soot from the fire made a thick, dirty, black covering on the walls and contents of the house.

The household utensils, pots, buckets and bowls were all made by hand of stone, clay, bark or skins, depending on what materials were available. The utensils were decorated with pictures of birds, animals or other symbolic designs with paints obtained from minerals or the juices of plants. Drinking cups were often gourds or bison horns, while spoons were made from wood or elk horns. Knives were common and were made of stone. Most tribes made fires by rubbing pieces of flint or sticks of hardwood together.

The tribes that lived by fishing made wooden items such as fish clubbers, fish spears, sealing shafts, whaling harpoons and raft like boats .From the fibers they wove nets and from bones they made hooks. From animal skins they made strips of sinew for their bows and fashioned snowshoes with which they could travel as far as 40 miles a day to catch deer and moose.

RINGS

For a long time the wedding ring was worn on the right hand and sometimes on the little finger because this digit was the least obtrusive. In many Eastern lands it has been worn on the thumb. What we now call the ring finger only gradually became the permanent choice for the symbol of matrimony.

Men, not women, were the first to wear rings. A Roman slave, when freed, wore a ring of iron. Gold rings were badges of citizenship. Pliny recommended the prevention of coughing and sneezing by shifting a ring from a finger on the left hand to the middle finger of the right hand. Gauls and Britons issued a code on ring wearing. The thumb was for doctors, the index finger for merchants, the middle finger for fools, the annular finger for students and the small finger for lovers.

The wedding ring has been a treasured symbol. An early ecclesiastic told why: "The form of the ring being circular, that is, round and without end, importeth thus that mutual love and heartfelt affection shall roundly flow from one to the other, as in a circle, continuously and forever."

THE CURIOUS CURFEW

How did the ringing of the curfew originate? William the Conquerer directed that all fires and lights be extinguished when the eight o'clock bell was rung. The law was repealed by Henry I in 1100, but the bell continued to be rung in many districts. The word curfew is derived from the French *couvre-feu,* meaning cover fire.

In the United States an ordinance establishing a curfew to keep young people off the streets at night has existed in Salem, Massachusetts, since Puritan days. Similar ordinances, providing that children under a certain age shall not frequent the streets after a certain hour, have been adopted in other cities.

CHEERS

Do you hobnob? Are you a hobnobber? If you have ever attended a social gathering where drinking took place and glasses were clinked together, you do and are.

Where did this curious habit of touching glasses before drinking start? People who fought duels in the past used to pause before their fighting long enough to drink a glass of wine furnished by friends. To make sure that no attempt was made to poison the wine in either cup, the habit of pouring part of the contents of each glass into the other was developed. This has continued up to the present time. Because there is no thought given now to the danger of poison, the ceremony of actually mixing the drinks has been omitted. Today we merely use the motion and touch the glass to show our expression of good will.

HISTORICAL HAIR—PART I

Hair is international! A clean shaven face was once the mark of a great nobleman or a prince because only they could afford such self-indulgence. Alexander the Great commanded his soldiers to clip off their whiskers because, he said, they would thereby remove the handle by which the enemy could seize them. Russia's Peter the Great, striving to make his barbaric nobles more suave and civilized, like the people of Western Europe, taxed the whiskers of his subjects and shaved off his own. In Ireland, a parliament at Trim enacted a statute in 1447 declaring that no man, unless he wished to be taken for an Englishman, should have a beard above his mouth. The upper lip had to be shaved at least every fortnight or have hair of equal growth with that on the lower lip. Daily shaving came into fashion in England during the Restoration (1660). Curiously, beards always disappeared when wigs came into fashion. When wigs went out and men wore their own hair, the mustache and beard began to appear again. Many times in history, laws have been passed prohibiting or requiring shaving.

HISTORICAL HAIR—PART II

The ancient Egyptians wore wigs partly for hygienic and religious reasons and also because of the hot climate. Their own hair was shaved or cropped to provide coolness while they were indoors. Wigs then gave them insulation from the sun outside. They preferred human hair, but sheep wool and palm fiber were also used.

In the 17th century, three European kings made wigs popular for men. Louis XIII of France wore a wig of natural hair, parted in the middle, and hanging to his waist. His son, Louis XIV adopted a wig when he began to gray. In England, Charles II began wearing a wig for much the same reason.

Both Queen Elizabeth and Mary, Queen of Scots, owned numerous wigs. The well dressed man of the Renaissance also put on a wig.

Throughout the 18th century the men wore wigs and those who could not afford them cut their hair in imitation of wigs. It was the colonists who brought the wig fashion to America, but by 1820 wigs went out of style for men.

BUTTONS, BUTTONS

Buttons have been used since ancient times. Museums have in their collections bone buttons older than written history. The Greeks used gold disks as buttons more than 4,000 years ago.

Buttons became popular as fasteners on clothing during the 1200s when fitted clothes replaced robes and loose garments. Up to that time, strings, girdles or pins usually served to hold clothing in place.

Long before buttons were used as fasteners they had significant decorative and symbolic value. Some ivory and metal buttons bore painted pictures. There were French buttons of porcelain. The Japanese made ceramic button

INVENTIONS AND DISCOVERIES
FROM PAPYRUS TO PAPER

The Egyptians gave to western civilization a method of recording information far more suitable than the cumbersome clay tablet of other peoples and developed a system of symbols—an "alphabet"—that made it possible to pass along ideas without face to face discussion. What was this idea that let man easily record ideas, stories, plans and information—and of course, cause man to learn to spell correctly?

At lease two thousand years before Christ, the Egyptians discovered that the river reed papyrus could be split into thin strips, flattened and pasted in layers to form a writing surface. By overlapping the edges they could form writing surfaces of almost any desired width and length. They wrote with a pointed reed as a pen and used ink made from water thickened with vegetable gum and darkened with soot. From the Greek word *papyr* we have obtained our word paper.

OUR MALADIES OF LIFE

In ancient Rome people sacrificed a red dog to Robigus, the rust god, for they thought that there was some connection between the dog star and epidemics of a rusty, red blight that often appeared on growing wheat and barley. The ancient Greeks made supplications to the corn goddess so that evil might be averted, and when the harvest was safely gathered in, they paid tribute with offerings of grain.

Not until the invention of the microscope in the 17th century was man provided with the means of determining the causes of plant diseases. Early investigators gazed into their microscopes and saw minute living organisms. What they discovered were tiny plants, bacteria and fungi.

The theory of spontaneous generation of disease was finally put to rest by the French chemist, physician and bacteriologist Louis Pasteur. His experiments showed that fermentation and putrefaction were the result of natural causes, the activities of microorganisms. Two new sciences were developed, bacteriology, the study of bacteria; and mycology, the study of fungi. The germ theory of disease was securely established and the road was clear to the conquest of many diseases that plagued mankind, his livestock and his crops.

In 1892, the Russian scientist Ivanowski discovered another causal agent of disease, in addition to, parasitic fungi and bacteria. He found that the sap of diseased tobacco plants with a peculiar mosaic appearance was infectious to healthy plants. It was still infectious after it had been passed through filters that held back bacteria and other known microorganisms. Other diseases of a somewhat similar nature were later discovered and it was shown that this kind of ailment was not due to microscopic fungi or bacteria but to an infection principle or virus.

Today, of course, many such maladies are known, and there seems to be no limit to their diversity for they plague almost every form of life.

HALF WAY TO THE STARS

Let's take a look at how the cable cars of San Francisco work. In principle nothing is simpler than to use a rope to pull a vehicle up a hill, but in practice, the cable car and its attendant machinery are a miracle of inventiveness. The connection between the car and the cable is an ingenious and most necessary device called a grip. The car moves when the gripman pulls back on the operating lever, closing a pincer like hold on the endless cable that is kept continuously in motion by electric motors in the carhouse. The grip itself is a semicylinder about one foot long and made of two parts that rehinge and close over each side of the cable like a vise. When the operator pulls back on the grip lever, a heavy, metal plate descends against this cylinder forcing the two curved hinges, or grip dies, to close around the cable. Two rollers, one on each side of the hinges, guide them over the cable. As a grip lever is pulled, pressure is put on the rope and the car is slowly put into motion, the tar on the cable acting as a lubricant to permit a smooth start and reduce friction.

That's how it starts but how does it stop? There are four separate braking devices on each car and both the gripman and the conductor share responsibilities for this phase of the operation. To operate the wheel brake, the gripman depresses a foot lever that activates a metal shoe which clamps down on the front wheels. The conductor also turns a hand lever on the rear platform to operate the rear truck wheel brake when descending very steep grades. The cable itself is actually a type of brake for when it is held tight by the grip, a descending car cannot go faster than its steady nine miles an hour. The track brakes are wooden blocks about two feet long, two inches deep and three inches wide which fit between the two wheels on one or both trucks of the front and rear chassis. The blocks, or track shoes, are in position over each rail and operated by the gripman using a large hand lever on the front end of the car. The blocks clamp down directly on the rail almost lifting the car up slightly and are quite effective as brakes. The blocks are cut from soft, clear pine and last about four days during summer months and two days during winter months when the wood soaks up moisture and wears out more rapidly. The emergency, or slot brake, is used only as a last resort. When the red handled, hot line lever is pulled it causes a guillotine like, tapered piece of metal 18 inches long and one inch thick to instantly penetrate the cable slot until it is wedged tight by pressure, friction and heat. It not only stops the car instantaneously but usually requires the services of a welding crew to burn it off.

THE CODE OF DOTS AND DASHES

The idea of transmitting intelligence by electricity over a wire, using a code of dots, dashes or hyphens and space signals, came to Samuel F. B. Morse in 1832. Although there is some question that Morse invented the idea of the telegraph he did build his first crude instrument in the winter of 1835 while teaching art and design at New York University in Washington Square, New York City. Later he built a 40 mile experimental telegraph line from the Capitol in Washington to Baltimore. It was over this wire that on the morning of May 24, 1844, he sent the historic first public telegram: "What hath God wrought!"

In 1846, the Washington-Baltimore line was extended to New York City by Morse and his associates. Morse also licensed others to build lines between New York and Buffalo, and Boston and other eastern cities. The telegraph grew as Morse persuaded the public to buy stock and finance it as a private enterprise.

THE PLYWOOD PLANE

"I didn't decide to take off until I actually did it. It felt so good I just took it off. The landing was really gratifying." These were the words of Howard Hughes in November, 1947, after he had piloted his huge plywood flying boat. He had taken the plane out into the harbor to make taxi runs. Alone and in shirt sleeves, Hughes suddenly turned up the great engines and, as a crowd of 1,000 looked on in amazement, lifted the monstrosity that many thought would never fly from the water—70 feet high and about a mile out of the choppy water.

The flying boat had become the subject of ridicule from the outset of its construction during World War II when it was given such nicknames as "Spruce Goose" and the "Flying Lumberyard." Its conception grew out of two plans by industrialist Henry Kaiser to combat the enemy submarine campaign—a squadron of large cargo planes to move men and equipment and a fleet of aircraft carriers to seek out and destroy the subs. Hughes pleaded for permission to finish his plane with his own money when the government determined the flying boat was no longer necessary. Its dimensions alone were, at that time, sufficient to cause hilarity. It had a wingspan of 320 feet, a fuselage 220 feet long and a tail 85 feet high. Its weight was 400,000 pounds. It had eight engines and was designed to carry 700 fully equipped combat troops.

A comparison of Lockheed's C5A transport, which was delivered to the military in 1969 amid controversy, is quite interesting. The C5A had a wingspan of 222 feet, a fuselage of 249 feet and a tail 65 feet high. It weighed 327,000 pounds and was designed for the same purpose—the transport of heavy loads of tanks and military equipment and troops.

INK AND PENCILS

It is thought that the first ink made in early times was a mixture of water and coloring matter from berries. Early in the history of China and Egypt, a durable black ink was made by mixing lamp black or charcoal with glue or various gums. When the ink was to be used, water was added. This ink is still used today and is known as India ink.

Ink is usually made by combining certain acids, a salt and water with a dye. Each ink manufacturer has his own formula. Formerly, the pigments were obtained from natural minerals but are now produced by chemists. The artificial dyes seem to have stronger, brighter colors and are cheaper. The ink used in ballpoint pens contains more dye than ordinary ink and is made by dissolving dye in certain alcohols. It has no water so it comes out like a thick syrup. Printing inks differ from writing inks. They are made by grinding the pigments into a solution of linseed oils and resins. The ink is thicker than paint, and varnish serves to bind the pigment to the paper.

As for pencils, it is true that our modern lead pencils do not contain lead. However, there was a time when they did. The Romans and Egyptians used lead in writing. But the true ancestor of our modern pencil was the all metal stylus used by artists and others during the times of the Italian Renaissance. The finest drawing tool these artists had was the silverpoint. However, this had to be used on a specially prepared surface. The idea of using lead with a wooden holder is mentioned in a writing of 1565. But, about this time, the mining of graphite started and it was realized this was a better substance than lead. In 1795, Conte first produced a pencil of modern type in which the graphite was mixed with clay, pressed into sticks and fired in a kiln. These pencils made a line which looked very much like the one produced by the older lead stylus.

POLITICS OF THE TYPEWRITER

In the autumn of 1867, Christopher Latham Sholes constructed the first typewriter in Milwaukee, Wisconsin. Charles E. Weller, a court reporter and friend of Sholes, agreed to test the practicability of the machine. In his *Early History of the Typewriter,* Weller says: "We were then in the midst of an exciting political campaign and it was then for the first time that the sentence was inaugurated. . . . and repeated many times to test the speed of the machine." Oh yes, the sentence: "Now is the time for all good men to come to the aid of the party."

ELEMENTARY

Two important incidents helped to set Pierre Curie and his wife Marie Curie on a lifetime search. William Conrad Rontgen had discovered rays of unparalleled penetrative power, which, in a talk before the Berlin Physical Society in 1896, he called "x rays." Shortly thereafter Henri Antoine Becquerel accidentally left a piece of uranium ore on a sensitized photographic plate and discovered that it reacted to the ore as if it had been exposed to light. Becquerel suspected an element at work that was more powerful than the uranium in the ore and suggested to Marie Curie that she search for it.

During the two years of chemically separating the constituents of a tone of pitchblende, the Curies isolated an element a hundredfold more active than uranium, which they called polonium. They continued separating constituents until they obtained from the mineral pitchblende a fraction of a gram of a salt of radium. In 1910, Marie Curie obtained metallic radium by electrolyzing a solution of radium chloride with a mercury cathode. The discovery of the radioactive power of radium and similar elements had far reaching effects in the fields of heat, medicine, atomic science and many others.

DIFFERENT OR THE SAME?

In 1635, John Winthrop the Younger, governor of Connecticut and an amateur mineralogist, came across a fragment of strange rock. It was sent by his grandson to London and in 1801, the English chemist Charles Hatchett, detected in the rock element number 41 which he named columbium in honor of the country in whose territory the mineral was first discovered.

In 1802, the Swedish chemist Ekeberg discovered the element tantalum. Because columbium and tantalum were chemically very similar, the English chemist William Hyde Wollaston decided in 1809 that the two were identical. If they were identical then Hatchett's name columbium should have prevailed since he was first. But Berzelius, Europe's leading chemist, thought Ekeberg's work more thorough and convincing and in 1814 voted against columbium and for tantalum.

In 1846, the German chemist Heinrich Rose showed that columbium and tantalum were two different elements. Because of their similiarity Rose called columbium niobium after Niobe, the daughter of Tantalus. The element kept its two names for many years— columbium in the United States and nibium in Europe. Later, however, an international conference of chemists decided to make niobium the official name of the element.

MEASUREMENTS

WHAT ABOUT GRAVITY?

The six bases of measurement are length, time, mass, temperature, electric current and luminous intensity. Each of these has a definitive unit of measurement. In length the meter is defined as 1,650,763,73 wavelenths in vacuum of the orange-red line of the spectrum of krypton-86. In time, the second is defined as the duration of 9,192,631,770 cycles of the radiation associated with a specified transition of the cesium atom. It is realized by tuning an oscillator to the resonance frequency of the cesium atoms as they pass through a system of magnets and a resonant cavity into a detector.

The standard for the unit of mass, the kilogram, is a cylinder of platinum-iridium alloy kept by the International Bureau of Weights and Measures at Paris. A duplicate in the custody of the National Bureau of Standards serves as the mass standard for the United States. This is the only base unit still defined by an artifact.

The thermodynamic, or Kelvin, scale of temperature used in the International System of Units has its origin or zero point at absolute zero and has a fixed point at the triple point of water defined as 273,16 Kelvins.

The Celsius scale is derived from the Kelvin scale. The triple point is defined as 0.01 degree C on the Celsius scale, which is approximately 32.02 degree F on the Fahrenheit scale.

In electric current, the ampere is defined as the magnitude of the current that, when flowing through each of two long parallel wires separated by one meter in free space, results in a force between the two wires (due to their magnetic fields) of $2 \times 10 - 7$ Newton for each meter of length.

The candela is defined as the luminous intensity of 1,600,000 of a square meter of a radiating cavity at the temperature of freezing platinum (2042 K).

ONCE UPON A TIME

Fact and fable are strangely mingled in the history of leap year. This once-in-four-years proposal privilege for women is not merely an unofficial tradition, but is based on actual legislation. It is said to have been started in Ireland by St. Patrick in the 5th century. In 1288, an act was passed by the Scottish Parliament in which "it is statut and ordaint that for ilk year known as lepe yeare, ilk mayden ladie, of baith high and low estait, shall hae libertie to bespeke ye man she likes." A few years later, a similar law was passed in France. By 1600, the custom had become a part of the common law of England. The legal books defined it: "As oft as lepe yeare doth return, ye ladyes have ye privilege of making love to ye men, which they doe either by wordes or lokes, as to them seemeth proper." A man who refused a leap year proposal had to pay a silk gown as a forfeit.

Leap years are a mathematical necessity, the extra dividend of one day which Father Time pays us every four years is a device of the astronomers to keep our years in step with the sun and the seasons.

There is a problem in assuming this will work out exactly, however. Instead of the year being 365 ¼ days or 365 days and 6 hours long, the true year was found to be 365 days, 5 hours, 48 minutes and 46 seconds in length. So the Julian calendar was 11 minutes and 14 seconds longer than the solar year. By 1582, this error had accumulated to 11 days. Then it was that Pope Gregory reformed the calendar to eliminate the accrued variance with the true year and so established the Gregorian calendar by decreeing that the day following Oct. 4, 1582, would be October 15. To keep the calendar in line with the solar year, he decreed the leap year should occur every year divisible by four except centesimal, or century, years which must be divisible by 400. Thus, the year 2000 will be leap year but not the years 2100, 2200 and 2300. The year 2400 will be and so on until the year 4000 which will be a common year, as will 8000 and every 4000 years thereafter. This further correction was necessary to eliminate a slight 26-second-a-year error still occurring. Thus, the calendar is now correct until the year 20000, when a leap year will be put back in to keep in line with the solar year.

FROM ONE DAY TO THE NEXT

The standard time zone system is based on the division of the world into 24 zones, each of 15 degrees longitude. The zero time zone is centered at the Greenwich meridian, with longitudes 7 ½ degrees W. and 7 ¼ degrees E. as its western and eastern limits and there is no difference in the standard time of this zone and Greenwich Mean Time. The 12th time zone is divided by the 180th meridian, sometimes known as the International Date Line. This is a hypothetical line that was fixed by international agreement as the place at which the calendar date changes by one day. Crossing the International Date Line to the west, the date is advanced one day; crossing to the east, the date is moved back one day.

EASTER AND THE MOON

Because of the variations in the days on which dates fall and the date of Easter, a person born on Easter Sunday may face a long wait until his or her birth date and Easter Sunday coincide again. A child born on Easter Sunday, 1962 – April 22 – will have an Easter Sunday birthday in 1973 and 1984 but not again in the 20th century. Easter Sunday can fall no earlier than March 22 and no later than April 25.

Easter falls on the first Sunday after the Paschal full moon. The Paschal full moon does not necessarily coincide with the astronomical full moon. The 14th day of the Pascal moon falls on or after the vernal equinox, which is arbitrarily designated as Marsh 21 for Easter computations. The Paschal full moon sometimes falls on a Sunday, in which case, Easter falls on the following Sunday.

DIGITS AND CUBITS AND PALMS, OH MY!

The average American automobile is about four cubits wide. Sounds Greek to you? Not quite; it's ancient Egyptian. The cubit was defined as the bent forearm from the point of the elbow to the tip of the middle finger of the outstretched hand. It was standardized to what is now 18.24 inches. The cubit was an instrumental measurement in building the Egyptian pyramids.

Also used by the Egyptians was the span, the distance between the tips of thumb and little finger of the outstretched hand—1/2 a cubit, or 9 inches. The size of a brick was 1 span x ½ x 1 nail—a nail being the length of the last two joints of the middle finger.

The palm was used by Egyptian merchants for measuring cloth. It was the breadth of four fingers, about 1/6 of a cubit or about three inches.

The digit was 1/24 of a cubit, or the breadth at the middle of the middle finger.

The fathom was an ancient Egyptian measure equal to the length of the outstretched arms—about six feet. It is still used in international nautical measurement.

The meridian mile—the unit used by seamen around the world—was established by 4000 B.C. as 4000 cubits or 1000 Egyptian fathoms.

BARLEYCORNS AND PACES AND FURLONGS, OH YES!

In 1324, England's King Edward II decreed that 3 barleycorns taken from the middle of the ear and placed end to end equaled 1 inch. King Alfred probably established the English foot as the measure of a cubical vessel containing 1000 Roman ounces of water. The lineal foot and the cubic foot were both standardized in this way.

The yard—three feet, or .50 fathom—was decreed by King Henry I to be the distance from the tip of his nose to the end of his thumb.

In 1500, the English mile was finally established in the following way:

3 barleycorns = 1 inch
12 inches = 1 foot
5 feet = 1 pace
125 paces = 1 furlong
8 furlongs = 1 English mile

In France, King Louis XVI was thinking about unifying the French measuring systems when the Revolution erupted. In 1790, the decimal metric system was imposed on the French, but Napoleon relaxed the law because of unfavorable reaction. Then in 1837, Louis Phillippe reinstated the system.

Today more than 80 per cent of the world's population uses the metric system.

BIOGRAPHY

SOCRATES

The Athenian philosopher Socrates was born in 469 B.C. His father Sophroniscus was a statuary; his mother Phaenarete was a midwife. In his youth Socrates followed the profession of his father. His physical constitution was healthy and robust. He was capable of bearing fatigue or hardship and was indifferent to heat or cold. He went barefoot in all seasons of the year, even during the winter campaign at Potidaea, and the same homely clothing sufficed for him in winter as well as in summer. He had a flat nose, thick lips and prominent eyes. He seems never to have filled any political office until 406 B.C., in which year he was a member of the senate of Five Hundred. At what time Socrates gave up his profession as a statuary we do not know, but it is certain that at least the middle and later part of his life was devoted to teaching. He never opened a school, nor did he, like the Sophists of his time, deliver public lectures. Everywhere – in the marketplace, in the gymnasia and in the workshops – he sought and found opportunities to awaken and guide boys and men in developing moral consciousness and knowledge. He died with composure and cheerfulness in his 70th year, 399 B.C. after drinking the fatal hemlock.

NOBEL

Alfred Bernhard Nobel, born in Stockholm in 1833, was a Swedish manufacturer, inventor and philanthropist. He was educated in St. Petersburg and the United States, where he studied mechanical engineering. He invented dynamite in 1866 and Ballistite, one of the first smokeless powders, in 1888. He is also credited with the invention of artificial gutta-percha and over 100 other patented items. His main wealth came through the manufacture of dynamite and other explosives in various parts of the world, and before his death in 1896, he bequeathed a fund of $9,200,000 to establish the Nobel prizes. They are awarded annually in several categories to a person or persons "who shall have conferred the greatest benefit on mankind." The awards were to be made without regard to nationality.

KEATS

The life of John Keats is almost impossible to believe. He was morose, despairing, frustrated, bitter and angry. His parents died before he was 11, his grandparents before he reached 14. His brother George left home and his brother Tom died of tuberculosis. In school he was hated and ridiculed by the other students. At 15 he was on his own. Somewhere in his tragic background, Keats acquired a love of poetry. For several years he was a recluse, studying hard for a poetic career. Then, when he was 21, he published his first volumes. They were greeted with critical disapproval, but Keats persevered and worked harder.

Keats' third volume of poetry justified his energy and ambition. At 23, he was the toast of Europe. He counted Shelley, Hunt, Lamb, Hazlitt and Wordsworth among his friends. But then fate dealt him a severe blow. *Endymion,* his most ambitious work, was condemned by some influential critics. In face of this rejection and despondency he labored harder than ever before—producing in one year at least eight poems that are among the glories of English literature.

This tremendous effort took its toll. Tuberculosis, exacerbated by Keats's exhaustion, won out, and a brilliant career was ended. A poetic genius was dead at 25. But in three short years, Keats had established his right to be in the vanguard of the greatest poets of all time.

FATHER SERRA

The father of the California Missions was Padre Fray Junipero Serra, the Apostle of California. Padre Serra was born at Petra on the Island of Majorca of peasant parents. He was baptized Miguel Jose. When he finished the University at Palma and entered the Franciscan Order in 1730, he took the name Junipero because of his devotion to Junipero, a companion of St. Francis. He was ordained priest on Sept. 15, 1731.

In 1749, he sailed for America to undertake missionary work in Mexico. Landing at Vera Cruz he traveled on foot to Mexico City. For many years he traveled over Mexico converting the natives. In 1767, he was nominated head of the missions of Lower California and two years later he was invited to proceed to Upper California. Serra reached San Diego and there on July 19, 1769, founded the first of the 21 missions which finally stretched along the coast for over 600 miles. He led the spiritual conquest of California and before his death at San Carlos Mission in 1784, he had baptized and confirmed more than 5,000 Indians and founded the first nine of California's Franciscan missions.

FIRST LADIES

Dolly Madison, as she was affectionately called, was one of the most popular First Ladies of the White House. She was beautiful and witty and knew the supreme art of making all her visitors feel perfectly at home. James Madison had few personal charms, but his wife made up for his weakness in meeting the public.

After her husband's death, Mrs. Madison lived in Washington, a block from the White House, and many a statesman, after calling on the new president, would pay his respects to "Queen Dolly." She died at 82, shortly after her last appearance at the British Embassy where she dined with Henry Clay and Daniel Webster.

Just the opposite of Mrs. Madison, Mrs. Pierce was a very backward and retiring woman who disliked public life and did not want her husband to become a candidate for the presidency. Some years before his nomination, Pierce had resigned from the United States Senate and returned to his New Hampshire home because his wife did not like living in Washington.

An interesting story about Mrs. Monroe during her husband's ministry to France at the close of the 18th century follows. A bloody reign of terror had broken out in Paris and many Loyalists were imprisoned, including Madame Lafayette, who was condemned to die. Mrs. Monroe, a very timid woman, whose husband had been an officer under Lafayette in the Revolutionary War, was ready to do everything in her power to save her. As the wife of the American diplomat, she was able to call at the prison. The meeting between Mrs. Monroe and Madame Lafayette was so touching that it affected the French authorities. The next day Madame Lafayette was given her freedom. She joined her husband in an Austrian dungeon. Later both visited the United States and were guests at the White House while Monroe was president.

ARISTOTLE

Aristotle the philosopher, was born at Stagira, a town in Chalcidice in Macedonia in 384 B.C. His father, Nicomachus, was a physician to Amyntas II, king of Macedonia and his mother's name was Phaestis or Phaestias. In 367 B.C., he went to Athens and there became a pupil of Plato, who named him the intellect of the school. He lived in Athens for 20 years, but left the city upon the death of Plato in 347 B.C., and went to his friend Hermias at Assos, where he married Pythias, the adopted daughter of the prince. In 342 B.C. he accepted an invitation from Philip of Macedonia to undertake the instruction of his son Alexander, then 13 years of age. His native city, Stagira, which had been destroyed by Philip, was rebuilt at his request. Aristotle spent seven years in Macedonia.

On Alexander's accession to the throne, in 336 B.C., Aristotle returned to Athens. Here he had the Lyceum, a gymnasium sacred to Apollo Lyceus, assigned to him by the state. He assembled round him a large number of scholars, to whom he delivered lectures on philosophy in the shady walks which surrounded the Lyceum, while walking around instead of sitting, which was the usual practice of the philosophers.

He gave two different courses of lectures every day. Those which he delivered in the morning were directed to a narrower circle of listeners, and included subjects connected with the more abstruse philosophy, physics and dialectics. Those which he delivered in the afternoon were intended for a larger circle and included rhetoric, sophistics and politics. He presided over his school for 13 years. During this time he also composed the greater part of his works. After the death of Alexander, Aristotle was looked upon with suspicion at Athens as a friend of Macedonia. He was accused of impiety but before his trial, he escaped from Athens in 322 B.C. to Chalcis in Euboea. There he died in the same year at the age of 63.

BLACKBEARD

Edward Teach, alias Blackbeard, alias Tach, Thach, Thatch and Teatch, was one of the most cruel of pirates. He wore a long, black beard in pigtails tied with ribbons over his ears. In action he wore slings over his shoulders holding three braces of pistols in holsters. He struck lighted matches in his hat to emphasize his ferocity. Born in Bristol, England, he became a seaman out of Jamaica. He teamed up with Captain Benjamin Hornigold in a career of piracy off North America and in the West Indies. After Hornigold surrendered, Teach formed a partnership with Major Sted Bonnet. He raided waters off Honduras, the Cayman Islands, Cuba, the Bahamas and the Carolina coast. Eventually he was pardoned for his crimes by Governor Charles Eden of North Carolina, who also married him to his 14th wife, a girl of 15.

Teach soon returned to piracy, plundering shipping in coves, sounds and rivers along the coast. Receiving no satisfaction from Eden, shippers appealed to Governor Alexander Spotswood of Virginia for help. He ordered out two sloops to hunt the pirate down. One, the *Pearl*, under Captain Robert Maynard, found Teach at Ocracoke Inlet, North Carolina, on Nov. 22, 1718. In the ensuing altercation Teach was killed and his head was cut off and hung on the *pearl's* bowsprit. Thirteen of his crew members were convicted in trials at Williamsburg, Virginia, and hanged there. It is said that after Teach's head was removed from the *Pearl*, it was set upon a pole at the Hampton River mouth as a warning to sailors. Today, this place is known as Blackbeard's Point.

NED BUNTLINE

The man who was largely responsible for the dime novel probably lived a life as adventurous as his characters. Edward Zane Carroll Judson, who became known to millions of readers as Ned Buntline, was born in New York in 1823. He ran away to sea to become a cabin boy. At fifteen he won a midshipman's commission for heroism. Four years later he resigned to serve in the Seminole Indian War, then went to Yellowstone for a fur company. At Eddyville, Kentucky, he set out after three murderers and captured two of them single-handedly. In 1846, he fought a pistol duel with Robert Porterfield and while on trial was fired upon in the courtroom by Porterfield's brother. He sprang through a window but was captured and jailed. That night, hanged by a mob, he suffered a broken neck but was cut down and smuggled back to jail. The jury refused to indict him.

He served in the Mexican War, and in 1849, led a mob that stoned the Aster Place Theater in New York. He was in prison for a year. Later, he served in the Civil War, became a sergeant and was discharged with a bad record. In 1896, he became friendly with Colonel William F. Cody, gave his the title of "Buffalo Bill," and began a series of dime novels that made Cody a national hero. Judson was married four times and went to his grave with twenty bullets in his body, sixteen of which he received in private shooting scrapes. He wrote more than 200 books and once turned out a 610 page volume in 62 hours.

SHAKESPEARE

The exact date of Shakespeare's birth is not known. The parish register shows that he was baptized in Holy Trinity Church, Stratford-upon-Avon, on April 26, 2564; and the world has for long chosen the date April 23 for the celebration of his birthday. His father, John Shakespeare, was a rising burgess of the borough, who in 1565, was chosen an alderman and in 1568, a bailiff.

Although no list of the pupils at the local grammar school survives, it can be assumed that young Shakespeare had the usual education of his time. This would emphasize Latin. A boy would learn to read, write and speak Latin fairly well and read some of the classical historians and poets.

William married at the age of 18. The Episcopal registry at Worcester, which preserved its records carefully, noted that a marriage license was issued on November 27, 1582. His wife, Anne Hathaway, was eight years older than he. Tradition associates her with the family of Hathaways who inhabited a beautiful farmhouse at Shottery, two miles from Stratford. On May 26, 1583, a daughter named Susanna was born and on February 2, 1585, twins were baptized Hamnet and Judith. The boy, Shakespeare's only son, died when he was 11.

How Shakespeare spent the years between 1585, and the time when he begins to appear in the London Theater records, is impossible to say. There are many stories but it is difficult to test their authenticity. We can deduce that for 20 years Shakespeare devoted himself assiduously to his art. He wrote more than a million words of poetry of the highest quality. He continued to look after his financial interests and he bought properties in London and in Stratford. We possess no letters written by Shakespeare. He made his will on March 25, 1616. It is a long and detailed document. He died on April 23, 1616.

RELIGION AND MYTHOLOGY

NEW WORLD BELIEFS

Some North American Indian mythology maintains that before the Indians came, the animal fathers lived upon the earth. The hills, rivers, forests, sun, moon, stars and winds were also here before the coming of the "two-legged walkers." Whole Indian clans were thought to owe their origin to animals and, consequently, they adopted the name of their creator. For instance, the Iroquois had clans named Beaver, Wolf, Turtle, Heron, Deer and Snipe. A figure of the animal served as the emblem, or *totem,* of the tribe. They also believed that not only birds, beasts and reptiles heard and answered their prayers; but that lakes, rivers and waterfalls were living spirits, who could hear the voice of man and who, in answer to prayers and offerings, would influence his life for good or evil. To many tribes the sun was a supreme spirit to whom they prayed and made sacrifices; many called for guidance upon the moon, stars and the Seven Spirits of the Wind. East, West, North and South were regarded as spirits with supernatural power. They thought the Summer-Maker and Winter-Maker were actual characters and they tried to keep the latter back by throwing firebrands into the air.

Some tribes said that lightning was the digging stick of the Great One Above and that when the lightning flashed and the earth shook, someone had disobeyed his orders. Thunder was regarded as a great black bird which made roaring noises when he left his home on the mountain peak.

COPTS

Copts are members of the Coptic Church of Egypt. The came *Copt* comes from the Greek word *Aegyptios,* meaning Egyptians. They descended from ancient Egyptians who were converted to Christianity in the first and second centuries A.D. The converts developed their own Coptic language and originated monasticism, which later spread to other churches.

At first, the patriarchate or ruling division of Alexandria was one of the most powerful in Christendom. But disputes concerning the nature of Christ led to a split between Room and Alexandria. The Egyptian church adopted a monophysite doctrine that asserted the single nature of Christ. In 451, the Council of Chalcedon condemned this doctrine as heresy. The Coptic Church broke away from Rome and Constantinople and remained independent under the patriarch of Alexandria. About 1.2 million Egyptians belong to the Coptic Church today. The church also has followers in Ethiopia, Jerusalem and South Africa.

STORIES OF THE STARS

It is probable that in most cases the ancient star gazers named the constellations in honor of their gods, goddesses and animals and not because the groups of stars looked anything like them. Most people think that the constellations are supposed to be pictures because they bear the names of objects, animals and persons. However, very few of the constellations look anything like the figures after which they were named.

The story which includes the greatest number of constellations is that of Andromeda. Her mother was Cassiopeia and her father Cepheus. Cassiopeia boasted that she was more beautiful than the sea nymphs who became angry and asked Neptune, the god of the sea, to punish her. He did so by sending Cetus, a sea monster, to lay waste the sea coast and to kill the people and cattle living there. Cepheus consulted an oracle and asked for advice. He was told that the only to appease the anger of Neptune and the sea nymphs was to sacrifice Andromeda to the sea monster. So she was chained to a rock by the sea to await her fate.

In the meantime Perseus was returning from his triumph over Medusa. This lady, like Cassiopeia, had been too boastful, saying that she was more beautiful than Minerva, the goddess of wisdom. Minerva changed the beautiful hair of Medusa into coiling snakes and decreed that any person who looked at the face of Medusa would be turned into stone.

So many stone statues sprang up that a rather serious traffic problem developed. Finally, Perseus, using his shiny shield as a rearview mirror and watching Medusa's image in it, backed up to her and cut off her head with his sword. From the blood of Medusa sprang the winged horse, Pegasus.

When Perseus found Andromeda about to be devoured by the sea monster, he turned it into stone by exposing it to a view of the face of Medusa which is marked in the sky by the eclipsing binary star, Algol. Thus, Andromeda was saved by Perseus and they lived happily ever after.

THE ORIGINAL SUPERMAN

There is no more celebrated hero in mythology than Hercules. He was the son of Jupiter and a mortal named Alcmene. He possessed high qualities of mind and character as well as great physical strength. Armed with a huge club, he preformed the famous Twelve Labors and many other remarkable deeds. Even when he was an infant and still lay in his cradle he strangled two serpents which Juno sent to destroy him. She was Jupiter's wife and was jealous of his love affairs and of the many sons he had by mortal women.

The death of Hercules was a traffic affair. When he and his wife, Deianira, came to the ford of a river, he placed her on the back of Nessus, a centaur, who carried travelers across for a fee. Instead of taking her to the other side of the stream, Nessus started off with her for the cavern where he lived. Hercules shot the centaur with an arrow. Before dying, Nessus told Deianira that his blood was a love potion which would enable her to retain the love of Hercules.

Later, when Deianira became jealous of one of Hercules' slave girls, she dipped one of his robes in this supposed love potion. However, it was a deadly poison and caused the death of Hercules soon after he put on the robe.

THE SCROLLS

In the spring of 1947, in the Judean desert above the shores of the Dead Sea, a young Arab goat herder, a Bedouin of the Ta'amira tribe, accidentally made a discovery of great importance to the history of Judaism and Christianity. This young Arab's curiosity about a small circular opening in the rocky cliffs near an old ruin called Khirbet Qumran, not far from Jericho, led to the discovery of the now well-known Dead Sea Scrolls.

The most frequently told story is that the boy chanced upon a cave as he chased a runaway sheep that had wandered from his flock. But the reason for Muhammad adh-Dhib's being at the site of the cave is of slight importance when viewed in the light of the discovery itself. For his entrance into the cave set off a history making chain of events.

It is entirely possible that the boy entered the cave in search of treasure, for the spot was well suited as a hiding place, lying in a remote area high above the shores of the sea. The cave did indeed contain a treasure but not the kind a boy of fifteen might expect. He found only clay jars. Some of the jars were broken, others whole, and from these he drew forth a number of scrolls made of leather and parchment, wrapped in linen and sealed with pitch. He took these scrolls to Muslim and Christian dealers in antiquities in Bethlehem, one of whom contacted a professor of archaeology at the Hebrew university in Jerusalem. The archaeologist immediately recognized the importance of the scrolls and the significance of their age and he managed to secure a number of them for the university.

In the meantime, the remainder of the scrolls, taken from the cave during the boy's visit, were turned over to a Syrian Metropolitan at St. Mark's Monastery in Jerusalem, and these later came into the hands of scholars at the American School of Oriental Research in that city. In this manner the documents from the collections of the Dead Sea Scrolls first came to the attention of scholars everywhere.

One of the first questions that scholars asked was the question of their date. To what period and to what century did these writings belong?

The story of how the age of the scrolls was determined is fascinating in itself. There are various criteria by which specimens of writing can be dated. One of these is paleography, the science of the evolution of the script. By comparing the script of the scrolls with samples of other early Hebrew script, paleographers placed the date at a period not later than 70 A.D.

There is other evidence that bears out this conclusion. The pottery, jars, textiles and coins found in the cave also permitted relatively accurate dating. The manuscripts were placed in these jars and put in the cave not later than the date when the settlement, found on the site of the discovery, was destroyed by the Romans. History records this as 68 A.D.

Final confirmation of the age of the scrolls came by modern scientific methods of dating with the use of radio carbon 14. A sample of the linen in which the scrolls were wrapped was subjected to tests with radio carbon 14. It was found that the flax from which the linen was made ceased to grow a certain number of years ago. From this information, it was determined it would mean a date between 167 B.C. and 237 A.D., allowing for a margin of error of 200 years either way. In any case, the results of tests with radio carbon 14 tally with the paleographic and historical findings and establish the Dead Sea Scrolls as belonging to the period between the first century B.C. and first century A.D.

LANGUAGE

WORDS, NAMES AND LETTERS

FROM A TO Z

Alpha and beta, the first two letters of the Greek alphabet, were joined together to form our word alphabet. In ancient Phoenicia, the letter A was called *aleph,* which meant ox. It was shown like a V with a slanted bar across it. The Greeks turned it upside down, which is the way we know it.

The letter G is thought to be the camel with its curved neck. It was called *gimel* in the Hebrew alphabet from which we get the source of gamma, the Greek name for G. From gamma and gimel it is an easy step to the word camel.

Phoenicians were great explorers and their word for M was *mem,* meaning water. This letter, shaped much like ours, represented the waves of the ocean. The letter Z was sixth in the ancient Greek alphabet. When the Romans thought they would have no use for it, they dropped it but later found it a necessary sound. By this time Z had lost its old position and had to be put at the end of the line.

CENSORED

Toward the end of the 18th century, it became impolite to mention the words *trousers or breeches.* Since it was obviously necessary to refer at times to these garments, various euphemistic terms were coined for the purpose. Trousers became *inexpressibles, inexplicables, ineffables,* or *unmentionables.* Later, when trousers regained their standing in polite society, it became imprudent to talk about undergarments, especially women's undergarments and these became unmentionables. Of course, modern advertising practice has, by now, removed all traces of prudery involving items of clothing. This has left unmentionables without a definite standing at present.

As a footnote to the above, the term *knickerbockers* for knee breeches came about more than a hundred years ago. Although the name of this garment is often credited to Washington Irving, it is really the British caricaturist George Cruikshank who started it. In the 1850s Cruikshank illustrated an English edition of the satire *A History of New York,* written by Irving in 1809 under the pseudonym Diedrich Knickerbocker. The garments of the alleged author, in these illustrations, and of his fellow Dutch burghers, led to the adoption of knickerbockers for knee breeches of any kind.

A DINOSAUR OF WORDS

Peter Mark Roget was an English physician who was born in 1779 and died in 1869. He liked to make lists of words as a hobby and to group them together when they were related to one another. Some were related because they were synonyms, such as grand and impressive; some because they were antonyms, such as dry and moist; some because they were reminders of one another, such as brother and sister. Altogether Roget made a thousand different categories of related words. Every word he knew or could find in the dictionaries was classified in one or more of these categories.

Roget's list of words was published in 1852. He called the book a thesaurus, or treasury, of words. Since that time dozens of editors, beginning with Roget's son, have revised the original *Thesaurus,* added to it and brought it up to date. Every edition is still called *Roget's thesaurus* in honor of the man who first had the idea.

TWO NORTHS

The names "Tarheel State" for North Carolina and "Flickertail State" for North Dakota are familiar to many of us. How did these names originate?

During the 1800s, North Carolina produced vast quantities of tar, pitch and turpentine. There is a story that, in one of the fiercest battles of the Civil War, some forces supporting North Caroline troops were driven from the field. The North Carolinians remained and fought it out alone. Later the routed forces greeted them by asking, "Any more tar down in the old north state, boys?" "Not a bit," was the answer. "Old Jeff's bought it all up." "Is that so? What's he going to do with it?" "He's going to put it on you'uns heels to make you stick better in the next fight." When Confederate General Robert E. Lee heard of the incident, he is supposed to have said, "God bless the Tarheel boys." Ever since, North Carolina has been called the Tarheel State and its people Tarheels.

The name "Flickertail" was suggested by the abundance in North Dakota of the Richardson ground squirrel or gopher. These animals are called flickertails from their habit of flipping or flickering their tails. "Flickertail" in this connection does not refer to the prairie dog, as is sometimes supposed.

HAIL CAESAR

In ancient Rome, a triumph was the highest honor that could be paid to a victorious general. The word triumph probably came from the Greek word *thriambos.* This was the name given to a ceremonial procession in honor of the god Bacchus.

When a victor was awarded a triumph, he entered Rome in a triumphal car drawn by four horses and proceeded along the *Via Sacra* (Sacred Way) to the Capitol. The victor, crowned with laurel, carried a scepter. The senators walked at the head of the procession. Next came trumpeters, carriages bearing the spoils of war, oxen to be sacrificed at the religious ceremonies and captives in chains. The general followed with his children and friends. The general's soldiers, cheering and singing as they marched, concluded the procession. In the triumph given to a naval commander, prows of ships and other nautical trophies were carried through the streets.

I'LL DRINK TO THAT

No one can say for sure where the story of spirits begins. Every civilization had its liquor. As Egyptian carving depicts distilling apparatus and shahs of India sipped liquors made from flowers in 800 B.C. Aristotle mentions liquor and legend has it that Alexander the Great passed the first loving cup as a peace gesture between Macedonians and Persians. It is said that the Aztecs greet Cortez with offerings of liquor. George Washington was one of the early American distillers. In both trade and war liquor figured in the early history of the United States. In fact, rum has been called the real spirit of '76.

The cocktail got its name at Dobbs Ferry, New York in 1777. In a burst of patriotism barmaid Betsy Flannagan served Washington's officers a special drink made from rum, rye and fruit juices, decorated by tail feathers from a Tory neighbor's plump rooster. Inspired, a French soldier in the group declared a toast: "Vive le coq's tail!" Thus, a legend began.

The word "whiskey" evolved from *uisge* or *usque,* both of Celtic origin. As early as the 12th century, the Irish drank *uisge beatha*; the Scots called it *uisgebah.* Either way the term means "water of life."

In the famous Whiskey Rebellion in western Pennsylvania, distillers went west to Kentucky. One of the first stills was near Georgetown, Bourbon County; and the product was called Bourbon County Whiskey.

A 17th century professor at Holland's Leyden University, experimenting with distilling, is credited with discovering *genievre,* French for "juniper," the berry that gives gin its flavor. The English shortened the name to gin. Both Russia and Poland claim to be the birthplace of vodka but its name stems from the Russian, meaning "little water." At one time vodka was made from potatoes but American vodkas are made from grains.

In the 1880s, in St. Louis, early railroaders used a ball on a high pole to signal engineers to speed up. This was called a highball. Trainmen, always on a fast schedule, only had time for a quick drink which usually was whiskey and water. They named it the highball.

PLANETS

All of the names of the planets in our solar system were borrowed from Roman and Greek mythology. The first six planets discovered were named by ancient star watchers. There has, however, been some confusion in naming planets discovered since the 18th century.

Mercury was so named because of its great speed. Venus was named because of its starlike brilliance. The red planet Mars was named for the fiery Roman god of war. Its two satellites are named Phobos (Fear) and Deimos (Terror). Jupiter was named after the chief of the gods no doubt because of its size. In mythology, Saturn was the son of Heaven and Earth. He became the father of Neptune, Jupiter and Pluto.

In 1781, Uranus was spotted by Sir William Herschel of England. He originally called his discovery "Georgium Sidium" in honor of King George III and it became known as "The Georgian" throughout Britain. In 1850, J. E. Bode renamed it Uranus in the classical tradition. Uranus in mythology was the earliest of the gods and was once called Coelus (Heaven).

In 1846, a new planet was discovered by the German astronomer Johann Galle although its presence had been deduced mathematically shortly before by England's John Couch Adams and France's U. J. Leverrier. In France the planet's name was proposed as Leverrier. Neptune, god of the sea, was accepted, however, to keep uniformity and also to bar nationalism.

In 1930, the present solar system was completed with the discovery of Pluto. Another son of Saturn, Pluto was god of the underworld and the dead. That name was probably selected because the planet is relatively close to Saturn and Neptune and also since it is the most distant and therefore still darkly mysterious.

THE FOURTH PROFESSION

The Fourth Estate is a name often given to the newspaper profession. The phrase is believed to have first been used in writing by Thomas Babington Macaulay. In 1828, he wrote in an essay that, "The gallery in which the reporters sit has become a fourth estate of the realm." He was adding a term to those already used for the three estates, or classes, of the English realm. These were lords spiritual, lords temporal and commons. The three estates later came to stand for government, while reference to a fourth estate described as any other influential body in English political life, such as the army of the press.

THE BIG APPLE

Why is New York sometimes called Gotham? How did New York's Bowery get its name? First things first. Gotham was the name of a town in Nottinghamshire, England, the inhabitants of which (about 1,200) were ridiculed for simplicity and shortsightedness and later were termed in derision "the wise men of Gotham." Washington Irving in his book *Salmagundi Papers* applied the name Gotham to New York, satirizing the shortsightedness of many of the inhabitants.

As for the Bowery, this old and wide street in New York City, extending northward from Chatham Square to the junction of Third and Fourth Avenues at Cooper Union, ran originally through part of Peter Stuyvesant's farm. The Dutch bouwerij, "farmstead," is from bouwer, "farmer."

NAME ORIGINS

Many of the loveliest geographical names come down to us from the first dwellers in our mountains, plains and forests.

Indian names often are musical and soft. Listen to the sound of Tuscaloosa, Shenandoah, Snoqualimie, Wyoming and Schenectady. Spanish priests and explorers gave towns long and beautiful names. Los Angeles was known as the City of Our Lady Queen of the Angels; Santa Fe was the Royal City of the Holy Faith of Saint Francis.

The Pilgrim Fathers, who set sail from Plymouth, England named their new home Plymouth. Around Massachusetts Bay the settlers named their towns Waltham, Cambridge, Bedford and Boston.

In New York State there are dozens of classical names—Troy, Athens, Carthage, Corinth, Ithaca, Rome, Syracuse, Attica.

Some towns were named for their principal industries—Oil City, Pennsylvania; Hershey, Pennsylvania; Ironton, Ohio; Gloversville, New York.

Among the picturesque and descriptive names there are Medicine Hat, Alberta; Tombstone, Arizona; Kicking Horse Pass in the Canadian Rockies; Badlands in the Dakotas; Hangtown; Rough and Ready and Dry Diggins.

Whatever their origin, these names and others show the imagination and activities of the people of Canada and the United States.

WHAT ABOUT THE HYPOTENUSE?

The Greek word for "angle" is *gonia,* and for "much" is *polys.* A closed figure containing a number of angles is therefore a polygon. The particular variety of polygon is named after Greek numbers: a five-angled figure in a pentagon – *pente* is "five"; an eight-angled figure is an octagon – *okto* is "eight"; and a six-angled figure is a hexagon – *hes* is "six". On this system a four-angled figure ought to be a tetragon and a three-angled one a trigon. Although these two terms are found in the dictionary, they are practically never used. The Latin equivalents are used instead: a four-angled figure is a quadrangle or a quadrilateral—*quattuor is Latin for "four"* – and a three-angled figure is a triangle – *tres* is Latin for "three".

A polygon with four equal sides is equilateral, from the Latin *aequus,* meaning "equal," and *latus,* meaning "side". The only equilateral polygon with a special name of its own is the equilateral quadrangle, which is a square if all angles are right angles or a rhombus if they are not. A triangle with three equal sides is an equilateral triangle; one with only two sides equal is an isosceles triangle. The word "isosceles" is derived from the image of a man's two legs standing apart, which forms an isosceles triangle with the ground.

CENSUS CONCENSUS

In the first United States census taken in 1790, the names of all family heads were recorded and posted in a prominent place in their community to help make certain of a complete count. Some of the names were colorful. They included Wanton Bump, Truelove Sparks, Sermon Coffin, Marcy Pepper, Booze Still and Boston Frog. Then there were such families as the Pockerpines, the Drips, the Fryovers, the Hungerpealers and the Slappys. In all, 27,337 different family names were recorded in 1790 in those states for which records still exist. Smith was the most popular with 5,932 families reported. Brown was second with 3,358 families. Then came Johnson, Davis, Jones, Clark, Williams, Miller and Wilson. These nine names accounted for about four percent of the white population in 1790.

The absence of middle names and middle initials from the 1790 census was because it was simply contrary to custom. Only three of the fifty-six men who signed the Declaration of Independence used middle names—Robert Treat Paine, Richard Henry Lee and Francis Lightfoot Lee.

Of the first names in 1790, the most noticeable trend was the contemporary preference for Biblical names. Family names fell into general groups that alluded to common events and experiences. These included such general groups as: Household and domestic affairs, involving such names as Fish, Trout, Tripe and the like; nations and places; human characteristics; family relationship; nature; the ocean and maritime subjects; property; war; death and violence and time.

WHAT ABOUT "A" AND "I"?

Palindrome means running back again and is used to indicate a word or sentence that is the same when read backward or forward. Level, radar, civic, tenet and noon are words which are palindromes. "Madam, I'm Adam" is a palindromic sentence. An unverified attribution to Napoleon is this: "Able was I ere I saw Elba." An interesting palindrome is a tribute to the man who completed the Panama Canal—"A man, a plan, a canal . . . . Panama." And here's another: "Name no one man." Latin gives us *si nummi immunis* (If you pay, you'll go free).

A REMINDER

Some of the loveliest of all legends are attached to the spice rosemary. This herb is for remembrance because, as folklore has it, once upon a time it bore a white flower which turned to the blue of the Virgin Mary's gown when she hung her linen on the bush to dry during her flight into Egypt. Shakespeare was cognizant of this for in Act IV, Scene V of *Hamlet,* Ophelia says: "There's rosemary, that's for remembrance."

Rosemary was also thought to strengthen the memory and was therefore an emblem of fidelity. This factor is said to have inaugurated the custom of wearing it at weddings. Rosemary, the leaf of an evergreen shrub and similar in appearance to a curved pine needle, has gathered legend after legend. One says that it will grow only in the gardens of the righteous; another, that it will not grow over six feet in height because it grew only to the height of Our Lord and after His death grew only in breadth.

THE THREE MONKEYS

Iwazaru is the one with hands over the mouth. Mizaru has hands over the eyes and Kikazaru has hands over the ears. Since these three monkeys are depicted in murals in ancient tombs in Nikko, Japan, they are sometimes called the Little Apes of Nikko, but generally, they are known in Japan as the *Koshinzaru.* They owe their existence to a play on the Japanese word *zaru,* meaning both "monkey" and "not." Actually, the proverb reads "nonspeaking, nonseeing, nonhearing."

In Chinese tradition, the proverb is credited to Confucius.

MONTHS AND DAYS

The history of names given to our months and days are good examples of new names for old. The Roman god Janus gave January its name. He was always shown with two faces, one gazing at the past and one looking to the future, a very fitting image for our first month. Before Julius Caesar, the Roman New Year began with March, the opening of the spring season for the waging of war, so the month was dedicated to Mars, the god of war. The opening of the spring bed gave us April. The Roman name was Aprilis, based on the Latin word *aperio* which means open. Since the Roman year originally started in March, September was their seventh month. The name comes from the Latin word *septem* which means seven. October, November and December were named from the Latin for eight, nine and ten.

The days of the week come from the following sources: Sunday was named for the sun; Monday for the moon; Tuesday for the Norse god of war Tiu (or Tyr); Wednesday for the Norse god Woden (Oden); Thursday for the Norse god, Thor; Friday for the Norse goddess Frigg, wife of Woden; Saturday for the Roman god (king-diety) Saturn.

CEMENT

How many people in the United States would associate the words *Portland cement* with one of the Portlands in the country? Mixed with water, sand and gravel or rock, it becomes concrete.

The cement was invented in 1824 by an Englishman, John Aspdin, who burned limestone and clay together. The mixture was ground into a fine powder. Aspdin called it Portland cement because, when hard, it was like a type of building stone found on Portland Isle, England.

A LISTENER'S PARADISE

Although the Great Seal of the United States and the Great Seal of the Treasury have Latin mottoes, it was sometimes difficult to carry on a conversation in old Latin when men spoke in sentences of 400 to 500 words. While one spoke all others had to sit by and listen until he had finished.

FEAR

The word *phobia* comes from the Greed word *phobos,* meaning fear. We all have heard of claustrophobia, a fear of being confined in a small area; or hydrophobia, a fear of water; or acrophobia, a fear of high places. But what about the hundreds of less familiar phobias? For example, a person who is afraid of snow is suffering from chionophobia and one who is afraid of gaiety is said to suffer from cherophobia. There is even a name for fear of the number 13; triskaidekaphobia.

LOOK IT UP

Have you ever considered the possibility that good spellers are born, not made? What happens to the college graduate, the company president or the military officer who spells atrociously and expects his secretary to make amends?

Next time you come across someone who really thinks he is good at spelling, ask him to spell the word for natural rubber, pronounced KOO-chook, and the word for pulmonary tuberculosis, pronounced TIZ-ic. If he says "Caoutchouc" and "phthisic," believe him.

As for spelling and pronunciation, you can ask what are the only two unrelated words in the English language that are pronounced like "sh" but spelled "su." If the answer is sure and surely, don't accept it. Only will a "sure" and "sugar" do.

By the way, "abstemious," "abstentious," "arsenious," and "facetious" are the only four words in the English language except for their derivatives that contain all five vowels in their proper order.

EXPRESSIONS

PART I

What is the origin of the expressions "stool pigeon," "taken down a peg." "to be blacklisted," "take a back seat," and "French leave?"

It was an old custom of hunters to fasten a captive wild pigeon to a stool and to move the bird up and down from a place of concealment in order to attract passing flocks of birds. Thus, "stool pigeon" came to mean a decoy or police spy.

The next saying comes from the British Navy. The flag used to be raised or lowered according to the prominence of visitors. The line was fastened by pegs, giving rise to the expression "taken down a peg."

"To be blacklisted" goes back to King Charles II of England, who listed in a black book the 56 men who had sentenced his father, Charles I, to death. They were all subsequently executed.

The fourth expression started in England. Members of Parliament belonging to the majority party got the front seats and those in the minority were left with the rear seats in the House of Commons and hence had to "take a back seat."

Most authorities believe that the last term, "French leave," can be traced to the 18th century French custom of withdrawing from crowded assemblies without taking leave of the host and hostess. Another possible explanation is that the word "French" is a corruption of the word *frank,* meaning "free."

PART II

What are the origins of the terms "red-letter days," "the jig is up," "make a clean breast of it," "battle royal," and "Adam's apple?"

First things first. Saint's days and other holidays were formerly and often still are marked in church calendars with red letters. From this custom comes the expression "red-letter day," meaning an especially fortunate or happy one.

"Jig" was first heard during Shakespeare's time and was a slang word for "trick," so the phrase simply meant that your trick or deceit had been found out.

"To make a clean breast of it" probably goes back to the ancient custom of branding a sinner on the breast with a symbol appropriate to the evil that he or she had committed. A person who confessed his sins would be one who had "come clean" or "made a clean breast of it." By confessing he had purged himself of sin.

The term "battle royal" came into existence when cock fighting was popular. Only two roosters were usually permitted in the ring but when a king visited the fight, four or more were put in the ring together. Today the expression denotes a fight among several people.

The popular name of the prominence in the front of a man's throat is called the "Adam's apple" from the story in the Old Testament in which the forbidden fruit lodged in Adam's throat.

PART III

One of the expressions associated with law is "as smart as a Philadelphia lawyer." This phase, meaning a lawyer of exceptional ability, grew out of Andrew Hamilton's defense of John Peter Zenger in New York City in 1735. Zenger, publisher of the *New York Weekly Journal,* had printed articles charging the British colonial government with corruption. He was arrested and charged with seditious libel. Philadelphia lawyer Andrew Hamilton brilliantly defended him. The jury's verdict of innocence was a great victory not only for Zenger but for freedom of the press in this country.

Another term relating to lawyers is "midnight judges." These were the judges appointed in February, 1801, by President John Adams in accordance with the newly passed Judiciary Act, which increased the number of federal courts. Because Adams, on the very eve of his retirement, filled the new places with Federalists and conferred the Chief Justiceship on John Marshall, an antagonist of President-Elect Thomas Jefferson, the incoming Republicans derided the incumbents as "midnight judges." They asserted that the judiciary had become a hospital for decayed politicians and replaced the act a year later.

SPACE AND EARTH

ASTRONOMY, GEOGRAPHY, GEOLOGY AND WEATHER

HERE TODAY, GONE TOMORROW

"Atlantis" and "Mu" are two words that have intrigued men for centuries. The legend of Atlantis dates to Plato or before. Plato wrote about a continent called Atlantis west of the Pillars of Hercules, the Gibraltar strait, that had disappeared 9000 years before. By coincidence the retreat of the last Ice Age took place about this time. Modern man has often tried to connect findings of submerged rocks in the Atlantic Ocean with a "lost people."

The Pacific version of the lost continent legend relates to the land of Mu which thrived in the splendor of the Pacific sun and one day was covered by the sea. As with Atlantis, many attempts have been made to trace the disappearance of this land.

For many years Easter Island was thought of as Mu because paved roads led down to the shore and into the sea. Later it was established that these roads had been used years before as landing ramps for native craft.

WHERE'S THE CHEESE?

To the unaided eye the bright surface of the moon is marred by vague dark areas. Through a low powered telescope these dark areas appear as smooth plains, so uniform that early astronomers thought that they might be seas. With more powerful telescopes the smoothness of the "seas" is found to be only relative. Other parts of the lunar landscape appear to be very rugged, with numerous mountains and other formations. The so-called seas, mountains, craters, rills and rays make up the principal features of the lunar landscape. Riccioli, an Italian astronomer who mapped the moon in the 17th century, named the craters for men of science. He also gave the seas such fanciful names as Mare Tranquillitatis (Sea of Tranquility) and Mare Serenitatis (Sea of Serenity)

Similarly, many lunar mountain ranges are named after ranges on the earth, such as the Apennines, Caucasus and Alps. The mountains are seen mostly in chains or groups, with single peaks as high as 29,000 feet. The Apennine range consists of some 3,000 peaks extending about 400 miles and rising some 18,000 feet above the Sea of Showers. A particular feature of the Alps is a great gorge, some 80 miles long and four to six miles wide. The rills are narrow crevices from as little as 10 to over 300 miles long, less than a few miles wide and of unknown depth. Although inconspicuous because of their width, over a thousand rills have been located.

In contrast, the rays are narrow streaks that are lighter in color than their surroundings and that radiate from several prominent craters, notably Tycho, Copernicus and Kepler. Since they cast no shadows, they can be neither ridges nor crevices. The rays that center on Copernicus extend hundreds of miles across the landscape. The most numerous of the lunar landscape features are the craters. As far back as 1878, around 32,000 craters were mapped. The craters are roughly circular in shape, with the floor generally lower than the surrounding plain. Many contain mountains rising from their floors; in others, numerous smaller craters are found.

TALK ABOUT THE WEATHER

On Feb. 9, 1870, President Ulysses S. Grant signed a joint resolution of Congress authorizing the establishment of a national weather service. Later that year, the first systematized, synchronous weather observations ever taken in the United States were made by "observer sergeants" of the Army Signal Service at 24 stations and telegraphed to Washington.

Today, thousands of observations are made daily by government agencies, volunteer observers, ships, planes, automatic weather stations and earth-orbiting satellites in an increasingly successful effort to answer the basic question: "What is the weather going to be?"

Actually, more than 200 years of weather observation and study in this country preceded the creation in 1870 of the Division of Telegrams and Reports for the Benefit of Commerce—the earliest name for the national weather service.

Only 24 years after the pilgrims landed at Plymouth Rock, the Reverand John Campanius Holm, a chaplain for the settlement near the present site of Wilmington, Delaware, began making systematic weather records. His diaries for 1644 and 1645 constitute the first continuous weather records in what is now the United States.

Thomas Jefferson and George Washington both had a real interest in weather studies. Benjamin Franklin was the first to study the progressive movement of a storm system as a whole.

During the War of 1812, the surgeon general of the army directed hospital surgeons to observe the weather and keep climatological records. The surgeon General's order was prompted by a growing interest in the effects of weather on health. By 1853, some 97 army camps were keeping weather records and many medical studies were based on these observations, including an investigation of the association of yellow fever with climate.

In 1849, Professor Joseph Henry of the Smithsonian Institution established an extensive observation net work by supplying weather instruments to telegraph companies. Simultaneous observations were made by local telegraph operators and sent to the Smithsonian. Maps prepared from these observations were displayed in Washington. By

1861, Henry had 600 stations making regular weather reports, but the coming of the Civil War broke up his network.

Increase A. Lapham, a Smithsonian weather observer, repeatedly urged the formation of a warning system for Great Lakes shipping. Finally, Representative Halbert E. Paine, a Republican from Wisconsin and a friend of Lapham's, introduced a bill in 1869, establishing a national weather service under the secretary of war.

YOUR LAND IS MY LAND

Not many years ago two continents were largely in the possession of much smaller independent nations.

Australia was colonized in 1787 by 750 reluctant convicts guarded by 250 soldiers. Most of the convicts were guilty of only trivial offenses, such as political agitation. Probably they would have rotted to death on the Thames had not Pitt's government been persuaded to transport them to the Botany Bay colony. Eventually their descendants acquired land, large-scale sheep farming was introduced and Australia prospered.

Africa then remained the only continent in which there were large tracts of land unoccupied by Europeans. By 1880, only the British and Boer settlements in the south, the Crown Colonies on the West Coast, a few Portuguese trading posts in Egypt, and the beginnings of France's African empire on the shores of the Mediterranean were in existence. The "scramble" for Africa began about this time with Germany, France, Belgium, Italy, Portugal and later Great Britain all hastening to stake out claims.

NOW YOU SEE IT, NOW YOU DON'T

One October morning in 1937, a German astronomer at Konigstuhl Observatory found a faint white line on one of the photographic plates exposed to the heavens the previous night. Obviously, some unexpected object was hurtling through the sky much closer to the earth than the slow moving stars. The length and curvature of the streak suggested to Dr. Karl Reinmuth that the object was an asteroid or planetoid—one of the baby planets that circle the sun along with their giant brothers. The evidence also indicated that the object was passing rather close to the earth. Additional observations found on plates at Johannesburg and Harvard told astronomers some interesting facts about this asteroid, which was named Hermes. They learned that it was about one mile in diameter. But the remarkable thing about Hermes was that it had passed within 500,000 of the earth. This put Hermes in the category of an astronomical near miss and made it the closest of all asteroids. One British astronomer estimated that in its future travels Hermes might even come within 220,000 miles of the earth, a bit closer than the moon. Unfortunately;, it has never been possible to check the accuracy of such computations by further observations of the asteroid. Traveling at its phenomenal speed, it was quickly lost in the far reaches of the solar system and has never been found again.

Hermes is by no means unique. The great majority of the little planets picked up at one time or another on photographic plates have also slipped from further view. This is true, for example, of both Adonis and Apollo, the second and third closest asteroids. Adonis was estimated to have approached within 1,376,000 miles of the earth in 1936, and Apollo came within 3,000,000 miles in 1932.

CAVE, SWEET CAVE

Caves have provided homes for man—especially during the Old Stone Age—for thousands of years. Some of the landmarks of cave archaeology are the discovery of Neanderthal man in a cave near Dusseldorf in 1856, the discovery of a similar skeleton together with worked flints in LeMoustier Cave in France in 1863, and the discovery of Peking man in a cave in the Dragon Mountains of China in 1921. Some of the Les Eyzies caves in Dordogne, France, were occupied for tens of thousands of years. The constant atmospheric condition of caves is an important factor in the preservation of the prehistoric cave paintings. The temperature of most caves is constant throughout the year, and is just a little below the average annual temperature of the area. Constant temperatures of 51 degrees F in Swildon's Hole, England; 52 degrees F in Wyandotte Caves, Indiana; and 54 degrees F in Diamond Caverns, Kentucky, have been recorded.

WATER

THE PRESIDENT'S CLOTHES

There are several stories about John Quincy Adams swimming naked in the Potomac during the days of his Presidency. He often walked from the White House at dawn on summer mornings, undressed on the riverbank, and dived in. In those days nobody thought much about it. If the President wanted to swim, that was his own affair and they respected his privacy. In one incident, however, on June 13, 1825, John C. Calhoun, the Vice-President, almost found himself a resident of the White House. Adams, 57 at the time, set out in a leaky canoe, procured and paddled by his French servant Antoine, to cross the river so that he might swim back. The craft foundered in midstream. Antoine, already naked, swam easily to the farther shore. Adams, wearing pantaloons and shirt, fought the heavy drag of his water-filled clothes and made shore only after a desperate struggle. He sent Antoine, dressed the Presidential pantaloons, to fetch dry garments and a carriage, and rode home vowing to be more careful in the future.

BREATHING WATER

Skin diviing is a relatively modern sport, although such people as the Polynesians have probably been at it for many centuries. Who actually developed the first crude goggles for the eyes is not known. However, the single lens mask or face plate came into being in the late 1920s. The Japanese were probably the first to fabricate a mask using a round pane of glass and a large piece of bamboo that was whittled to fit the forehead, cheeks and under the nose.   In 1938, the first rubber masks were manufactured in Japan. About the same time, Owen Churchill, an Olympic yachting champion observed the divers in the South Pacific using reed type mats laced to their feet to give them additional thrust in plunging down in search of fish.   On his return to the United States, Churchill started producing what he called "swim fins." Then in 1943, Emil Cagnan and Jacques-Yves Cousteau of France developed a breathing appliance that was attached to a tank of compressed air, usually strapped to the back and having no lines to the surface. It was named the "aqualung." Skin diving employs a mask and fins and may use complete scuba—self-contained underwater breathing apparatus—equipment.

TO AND FRO

Although rowing has always been considered as consisting of rapid movement, there was one time in history when this notion was in question. The Greeks, Romans and other medieval navies used a Bireme, a long rowing ship propelled by two banks of oars, one above the other. This peculiar arrangement of oarsmen on two levels within the hull, often separated by a partial deck, once gave rise to an odd predicament. Christian Crusaders, fighting to wrest the Holy Land from the infidel Turk, had besieged the Palestinian coastal city of Acre in 1189. Their blockading fleet was engaged by a Turkish fleet. In the ensuing ramming and grappling, Turks managed to get aboard one bireme and sweep out most of the top oarsmen. They grabbed the upper oars and began rowing in order to make away with the vessel. Below deck, the lower oarsmen countered mightily. With the Turks pulling in one direction and the Christians the other, the ship slewed back and forth and churning foam before remaining crusader warriors in the ship regained control.

THE AMAZING AMAZON

A Noted traveler described the Amazon water system as more like a moving sea than a river, more like the Mediterranean than the Mississippi. Ocean going vessels can cruise up the Amazon as far as Iquitos in Peru, 2,400 miles from the Atlantic Ocean. The river there is 120 feet deep. Even 400 miles farther up river the Amazon is still as wide as the Mississippi at New Orleans.

This huge water system drains an area much larger than all of Europe. Most of the basin is so flat and the smaller tributaries so numerous that a diagram of the river looks like the circulatory system of the human hand with all its capillaries.

THE SEEING SHIPS

To the old-time sailing men, their ships were so important they felt almost alive. The beginning of ship decorating and figutreheads seems to have been in Egypt or India. At first an eye was painted on the bow. The simple seafarers of that day felt the ship would be better able to spy out a safe course. The Greeks and Romans also followed this custom and elaborated on it by placing statues in parts of the ship. It is thought that the habit of displaying the female figure may have come from the Greek Athenians, using a statue of the goddess Athena on the bows of their ships.

The famous "Winged Victory" set up on land to celebrate naval victory shows how a figure can symbolize the forward movement of the ship. In Renaissance days, ships were covered with carvings to bear witness to the wealth and power of the nations to which they belonged. A beautiful figure was thought to bring good luck to the ship and so individual ship owners came to include a figure or half figure, even if they couldn't afford other carvings. To many old seamen, shipping on a vessel without a figurehead would have been unthinkable.

JURISDICTIONS

Territorial waters apply to that part of the open sea over which a nation can claim jurisdiction. In the past it was generally conceded that this consisted of a belt of coastal water one marine league or about three and one-half statute miles wide, measured from the low water line.

Bays or arms of the sea are usually considered entirely within the jurisdiction of a nation even though the entrances are more than two leagues across.

The "three mile limit," when adopted, coincided with the maximum range of existing coastal defense cannons. The three marine mile definition of coastal waters was formalized in a treaty between the United States and Great Britain signed January 23, 1924.

That treaty also gave the United States certain conditional rights of search or seizure over private vessels flying the British flag when within an hour's sailing distance from the coast of the United States or its possessions. This distance is popularly referred to as the twelve mile limit, whose use has continued to the present with several nations recognizing the rule as law.

SAILING BACKWARDS

The origin of the terms starboard and port dates back to the Viking ships. These ships were fitted with one rudder—a long, straight blade, controlled by a tiller slotted at right angles into the rudderhead. Since the tiller was located on the right side of the stern, the steering side came to mean the right side of the ship. "Starboard" is a corruption of the "steer board." Since the crew always tied up the ship in port with this rudderless side against the quay, it is obvious that the "port" side is the left one. The loading side where cargo was received, became another term for the left side—"larboard."

Although square rigged ships are not in vogue today, they could do something which the most efficient present day America's Cup yacht can't do. They could sail backward. This ability, convenient for docking in harbors, once saved a famous square-rigger at sea. On a trip between Liverpool and New York with a load of immigrants, the Atlantic record holder *Dreadnaught* ran into a February storm and lost her rudder. She was helplessly swept sideward and trapped in the wave troughs with her nose pointing north. But the nearest refuge was the Azores, off to the south. Therefore, the captain swung the yards around and sailed her backward for more than 200 miles. Going stern first she made the respectable rate of 4 mph.

WATCHES, BELLS AND DOGS

Ship's bell time originated in sailing ship days when the crew of a vessel was divided into port and starboard watches, each on duty four hours, then off four hours. One stroke on the ship's bell indicates the first half hour of the watch. Then an additional bell is struck for each succeeding half hour. Thus eight bells indicate the end of a four hour watch. This is repeated each watch. When the time calls for two or more strokes, they are sounded in groups of two.

The first five watches are as follows: first watch, 8:00 p.m. to midnight; middle watch, midnight to 4:00 a.m.; morning watch, 4:00 to 8:00 a.m.; forenoon watch, 8:00 a.m. to noon and afternoon watch, noon to 4:00 p.m. The next four hours are divided into two dog watches—the first dog watch, 4:00 to 6:00 p.m.; and the second dog watch, 6:00 to 8:00 p.m. By means of the dog watches, the watches can be changed every day, so that each watch gets a turn of eight hours rest at night. Otherwise each member of the crew would be on duty the same hours every day. In the second dog watch, to indicate that a new watch has taken over, the sequence of bells is varied as follows: one bell, 6:30 p.m.; two bells, 7:00 p.m.; three bells, 7:30 p.m.; eight bells, 8:00 p.m. The ship's clock repeats the sequence of one to eight bells every four hours day and night without variation.

THE WILIWILI

It is generally believed that the Polynesians brought the sport of surfing to Hawaii and were the first to surf. There is evidence in Peruvian artifacts that the Incas also did a great deal of surfing on the beaches near Lima.

Among the ancient Hawaiians the greatest surfers were the chiefs and kings. Their boards, fourteen to eighteen feet long and weighing up to 150 pounds, were constructed from a rather limited supply of wiliwili wood. The heavier koa wood was passed off on those of lesser rank.

The modern sport of surfing was revived when Alexander Ford founded the Outrigger Canoe Club in Hawaii in 1908. Until the 1940s the sport developed slowly.

Fiber glass and galas wood fiber surfboards were produced in the 40s but with the perfection of the hard plastic foam surfboards in 1957, surfing boomed.

THE DUTCHMAN

The *Flying Dutchman* is a phantom ship identified with stormy weather off the Cape of Good Hope and thought to forebode ill luck. According to one form of the legend the ship is doomed never to enter a port because of a murder committed on board; another says that the captain, a Dutchman, swore a profane oath that he would weather the Cape though he should tack there till the last day. There he and his ship still fight but never succeed in rounding the point. He sometimes hails vessels and requests them to take letters home. The legend is supposed to have originated in the sight of a ship reflected from the clouds. It has been made the groundwork of one or two novels and an opera by Wagner.

BUOYS

Buoys are the sailor's traffic signs. Even without printed directions they tell the navigator what he should know. Their colors, shapes, numbers and sounds direct boats and ships safely along the waterways.

The sailor's chart identifies the type of buoy he is passing. When entering a harbor from the sea, red buoys mark the right hand side of the channel; black buoys the left hand side. Buoys striped with alternate bands of black and red indicate an obstruction. A buoy marked with alternate black and white vertical lines indicates the middle of the channel. A white buoy marks a place where boats can anchor.

Can Buoys look like cylinders or cans with flat tops. Nun buoys are shaped like the headdress of certain orders of nuns. Wooden or steel poles sticking out of the water, usually at a slant, are called spars. Can buoys are usually painted black, nun buoys red and spars may be either color.

Buoys on the right hand side of the channel have even numbers and those on the left odd, increasing from seaward toward the head of navigation.

Lights on buoys may be fixed or flashing. They also may make a bell ring or a whistle or gong sound.

SPORTS

SPORTS HISTORY

RINGS, COLORS AND WORDS

The rings or circles which form the Olympic symbol originally represented the five major continents—namely Europe, Asia, Africa, Australia and America (both North and South). However, true concept is that the rings are linked together to denote the sporting friendship of the peoples of the earth, whatever their creed or color. The colors for these rings are chosen because at least one of them—blue, yellow, black, green and red—appears in the flag of every nation of the world.

The Olympic flag, which appeared at Olympic competition for the first time at Antwerp in 1920, has a white background with no border. In the center are the five rings. The words "Citius, Altius, Forthius," which appear under the circles, were conceived in 1895 by Father Didon, head master of the Arcueil College near Paris, while delivering a speech glorifying the athletic achievements of his pupils. The words mean "faster, higher, stronger," indicative of the competing athlete's endeavor to run faster, jump higher and throw more strongly.

UNLIMITED FOOTBALL

Legends connected with football in early England are many. At Derby, where football has been played for centuries, there was the story that the game was a memorial for a victory over the Romans in the third century. Fritz Stephen, who wrote in the twelfth century, refers to a game unmistakably football which was played annually on Shrove Tuesday. When Edward II was king, football was popular in London but unpopular with merchants whose windows were broken and sons were hurt playing the game. It had no limits as to the number of players nor did it have any bounds with regard to its brutality. Contemporary sources credit it for thousands of deaths.

In 1314, Edward II forbade football. Richard II and Henry IV both passed statutes against the game. Henry VIII was even more strict. Yet the game thrived and many prominent and powerful friends of football point out its tremendous military value. It might be said that the ruggedness of the English in many wars they fought during this period is traceable to their most popular but illegal game of football.

The game as played during this period was flexible and simple. Goals could be two bushes, posts, houses or towns, from a few score yards to a few miles apart. The ball was placed midway between the goals. Each team consisted of the same number of players from twenty to several hundred. When confined to a street or field of play, this was the origin of what became known as the Rugby Union Game. Queen Elizabeth I cared little for football although it was mentioned any number of times as the developer of stamina for war and privateering. Football survived not only the edicts of kings and queens, but also Puritanism, and remained the favorite sport of both the people and the soldiers of England to the beginning of the seventeenth century.

THE TRAVELING PUCK

The National Hockey League was born in Montreal on November 22, 1917. Representatives from two Montreal teams, one club from Quebec and one from Ottawa, laid the cornerstone. When play actually started on December 19, the Quebec franchise was in limbo, but the Toronto Arenas joined to even off the schedule. By 1925, three American teams had become part of the league. New York and Boston became mainstays while the Pittsburgh club transferred five years later to Philadelphia. After one year in Philadelphia it too left.

Inclusion of three more American entries in 1926, brought the league to ten teams which was divided into two divisions, Canadian and American. The Chicago Black Hawks, New York Rangers and Detroit Cougars made their debuts. The league now had two New York franchises with the original, the Americans, in the Canadian division. By the late 1920s the league was an eight team loop. Shortly before World War II the league melted to six teams. The Montreal Maroons, who had hung on for 14 years, called it quits. The Brooklyn Americans, formerly New York, followed on their heels. The six team league stood unchanged until 1967.

GOFF

The following is an excerpt taken from *The Sports and Pastimes of the People of England,* by Joseph Strutt, 1801.

"Goff, according to the present modification of the game, is performed with a bat not much unlike the bandy; the handle of this instrument is straight and usually made of ash, about four feet and a half in length; the curvature is affixed to the bottom, faced with horn and backed with lead; the ball is a little one, but exceedingly hard, being made with leather and stuffed with feathers. There are generally two players who have each of them his bat and ball. The game consists in driving the ball into certain holes made in the ground, which he who achieved the soonest, or in the fewest number of strokes, obtains the victory. The Goff lengths, or the spaces between the first and last holes, are sometimes extended to the distance of two or three miles; the number of intervening holes appears to be optional, but the balls must be struck into the holes and not beyond them; when four persons play, two of them are sometimes partners, and have but one ball, which they strike alternately, but every man has his own bandy."

RUGBY – THE BIRTH

At the famous Old Bigside School in Rugby, England, a revolutionary incident happened purely by chance and on the spur of the moment one late afternoon in 1823. It seems that the rules of the Old Bigside School required that all games end promptly on the stroke of the 5 o'clock bell.

On this particular afternoon it appeared that the game would end in a scoreless tie. Just as the school bell resounded on the first stroke of five, a long sailing punt was sent down the field, the last effort of one side to make a score. Suddenly out of the mass of fifty players on the other side sprang a young Rugberian by the name of William Webb Ellis. With arms outstretched he caught the ball, but instead of heeling it and then taking a free kick, with the inspiration of desperation and contrary to rule and custom, he put the ball under his arm and set sail for the goal. With his arms free, he zig-zagged in and out and cleared the pack, crossing the goal line just as the last stroke of five came sounding over the field. This maneuver was deplored as unfair, improper and unbecoming a gentleman. Such was the feeling at the time, but it wasn't long before the sense of outrage changed to a feeling that maybe the bold and revolutionary youth had a good idea in his unorthodox behavior. This breach of the rules led in time to the adoption of the feature of running with the ball, and so originated the game of "Rugby."

The exploit and the name of the tradition-defying lad are preserved on a tablet placed in a wall at Rugby. The inscription reads: This Stone Commemorates the Exploit of William Webb Ellis who with a fine disregard of the Rules of Football, As Played In His Time, First took the Ball in His Arms and Ran With It, Thus Originating the Distinctive Feature of The Rugby Game A.D. 1823.

A ROUGH GAME

Although lacrosse is an interesting and enjoyable spectator sport, one game in history had much more of an impact on its viewers than they bargained for. In 1764, a lacrosse game took place outside Fort Michilimackinac in northern Michigan between teams of Chippewa and Sac Indians. It was a gala holiday event to celebrate the birthday of King George III and the garrison of 40 English troops and several fur traders lounged outside the open gate to watch the contest. The two teams with more than a hundred loin-clothed Indians on each side, ran whooping and slashing after the ball as it flew back and forth. During the play the ball was thrown into the spectators. The contestants surged after it. Their squaws, who had been cheering from the sidelines, closed in and handed tomahawks and knives from under their blankets to the players. Immediately they fell upon the white men, slaughtering more than half of them, making prisoners of the rest and looting the fort and its stores.

A GREAT DAY FOR BOWLS

There seems to be no evidence of the exact beginning or origin of the game of Lawn Bowls. The Southampton Old Bowling Green, established prior to 1299 A.D., is the oldest in the world. It was partially destroyed in World War II, but was reconstructed and preserved by funds received from all over the world. In July 1588, Sir Francis Drake was playing the famous game on Plymouth Hoe, when it is reported that while he was engaged in Lawn Bowling he was approached by an excited courier with the information that the Spanish Armada was approaching the shores of Britain. To this courier he replied, "They must wait their turn, good Souls," and he stooped and finished his game.

The history of lawn bowling in the United States is not quite clear. Many historians believe that in 1615, the game was active in Massachusetts and Connecticut. It is definitely known that there was a Bowling Green on the estate of George Washington at Mount Vernon. At about this time bowling on the green was active in New York City and Williamsburg, Virginia. The game was practically nonexistent for about 100 years following the Revolutionary War. The American Lawn Bowling Association was organized in Buffalo, on July 27, 1915.

BONES AND POLES

Before and during the Middle Ages people used animal bones to ice skate. Tied underfoot, these were hard enough to slide upon, but their roundness gave no bite for striding. The skater moved by shoving himself along with a metal-picked pole. It was crude and laborious sport.

Some young English skaters of the thirteenth century, realizing that they carried what amounted to a knight's lance, took up jousting. Two opponents would push to high speed and glide together with poles held forward. The jolt was often disastrous. A chronicler of the period noted, "One or both do fall, not without hurt; some break their arms, some their legs, but youth, desirous of glory, in this exerciseth itself against the time of war." With the invention of iron blades, the pushing pole was eliminated from skating since the edged metal blade provided it own traction.

FROM PRISON TO SQUASH

The sport of rackets was evolved in English jails, notably the debtors' prison, the Fleet. In 1820, Robert Mackay, a debtor, became the first accepted champion of a sport which was quickly adopted by the public schools. When Sir William Hart Dyke won the championship in 1862, he was the first holder of the title who had not learned the game in prison. Squash rackets, played with a soft ball and in a smaller court, began as an off shoot of rackets and was also adopted by the public schools. It grew quickly in popularity though its extent was limited by the number of courts.

ORIGINS

What is the origin of badminton? Where did handball originate? How did the term derby in horse racing originate? Why is the square in which boxers fight called a ring? First things first.

Badminton is a present day version of an earlier and simpler game called battledore and shuttlecock. British officials in India learned the game and took it to England. There it was played at Badminton, Gloucestershire, the country home of the Duke of Beaufort. It was here that the game took its present name.

Handball probably originated in Ireland in the 900s or 1,000s. Irish immigrants introduced the game into the United States in the late 1800s.

The derby event is an annual horse race held on the famous race course at Epsom, England. It was started by the Earl of Derby in 1780. Only three year old horses are admitted. In imitation of the English race, there are the Kentucky Derby in the United States and the French Derby in France.

Early rules in boxing called for a circle, 5 feet in diameter, to be drawn in the middle of the arena. Fighters were supposed to start with their toes outside that ring.

GYMNASTICS

The early Greeks spent as much time on gymnastics and athletics as they did on music and art. Physical training played a part in medicine, but even before the time of Hippocrates, Greek physician and father of medicine, it was prescribed to counteract the ill effects of luxurious living. They believed that physical training could, within limits, increase the size, strength and aptitude of the human body and gymnastics, therefore, sought to exercise all parts of the body. They believed that general physical development improved the coordination of mind and body.

The gymnasium and gymnastics both played an important role in Plato's Republic and in some works of Aristotle. Homer's *Illiad* makes the earliest mention of gymnastic sports and athletics, describing how Achilles began a series of games in honor of Patroclus and gave prizes to the winners in boxing and wrestling. The Spartans were probably the greatest enthusiasts of gymnastic training. The state erected gymnasiums and demanded prescribed physical exercise for both male and female youths.

IS IT CRICKET?

Although cricket clubs as such were few prior to 1750, members of social clubs often played. In those days the dress for cricketers was not very different from a person's normal attire—tight breeches, silk stockings and buckled shoes, full sleeved shirts and neat jockey caps. The umpires wore laced cocked hats and full skirted coats and each carried a cricket bat which the batsman, when running, had to touch to make good his ground. The striking end of the bat was curved like an old fashioned dinner knife. It was of one piece and it defended a wicket of two stumps and one bail on a pitch, most often rough and bumpy, twenty-two yards long—as it is today. All bowling was underarm, along the ground and generally quite fast. Pads and gloves were unknown. The scorers notched or carved the runs on sticks. But even by the 1740s, a code of laws was in use that was not so very different from that used today. Cricket had already paved the way as England's premier game.

ON GUARD!

Like boxing, wrestling, archery and javelin throwing, fencing became a sport only after it stopped being deadly combat. Gladiator schools in ancient Rome were the first fencing schools. But real fencing science dates back from the time gunpowder and bullets made heavy armor and armor-cracking weapons obsolete. Lighter thrusting swords, such as the rapier, which could be manipulated with one hand, appeared and commanded immediate respect.

As swordsmen grew more confident of their ability to fence and parry with the lighter weapons, they gave up the parrying shield or buckler they had carried in the left hand, and abandoned the boxer's crouch in favor of a profile *en garde* position which offered the smallest target possible. In the second half of the sixteenth century, fencing reached a milestone, the lunge. It was discovered that the reach could be increased by advancing the front foot in a long step forward while holding the back foot stationary.

TENNIS, ANYONE?

One of the earliest of all ball games, court tennis has remained largely unaltered for more than 700 years. This game, from which lawn tennis was derived, was called "royal" or "real" or "court" tennis. Although it was a popular game from the fourteenth to the nineteenth century, by the middle of the twentieth century it had a very small following, limited to membership in a few exclusive clubs in England, France and the United States.

Today's tennis courts are prohibitively expensive. The oldest one in the world is one that Henry VIII had built at Windsor Castle in 1529. A court today measures 110 feet by 38 feet with a skylight 30 feet overhead. The four walls and floor are made of cement. Among the features of the court are a roofed shed, running around three sides of the court and the tambour. As in lawn tennis, a racket and a felt covered ball are used. A net divides the court at the middle and the scoring is similar to that of lawn tennis. But there are many important differences and some call the game one of the most complicated in the world.

Two of the greatest players developed in the United States were Jay Gould, amateur champion from 1906 to 1926, and Tom Pettitt, a professional. After 1928, the game was dominated for many years by Pierre Etchebaster, a French Basque livi8ng in the United States.

BALLS AND PINS

Historians of the sport of bowling have assembled many interesting facts. Stone age artifacts indicate that a very crude form of the game existed in prehistoric times. Apparently, men rolled rounded stones at animal bones or at pointed rocks which were placed on smooth ground. Specific evidence of the sport can be traced to ancient Egypt. Objects used in bowling have been found in the tomb of an Egyptian child. By 300 A.D. a form of the game had established itself in Northern Europe, where it was believed that the skill of a person at bowling was proof of his religious purity.

From Northern Europe, bowling found its way to England. It was widespread in Henry VIII's time, when it was played on both wood and clay lanes. It was also played as "Lawn Bowls" and was a favorite of such heroes as Sir Francis Drake who, it is said, finished a game of bowls before setting sail for his famous victory against the Spanish Armada in 1588. Certainly there were many derivations of the sport from the Italian boccie to the game of ninepins played in Holland but virtually all of them kept the basic principle of rolling a ball at pins.

The Dutch brought the game to the New World. By the 1800s, betting was quite common among the participants. There was a drive that finally led to the games being outlawed about 1842, first in Connecticut and then in New York. If the game of ninepins was illegal, the game of tenpins wasn't and the sport has been growing throughout America ever since.

OLD BARNEY

On a warm June afternoon in 1903, a man named Barney Oldfield stood alongside his spanking new race car "999." His mechanic, a man named Ford, made a few final adjustments to the streamlined motor. Oldfield climbed behind the wheel. Then he sped bumpily off on the Indianapolis race track and became the first man to drive a car a mile a minute.

After the historic event, Oldfield announced firmly, "No man will ever go faster than 60 miles an hour. At that speed the air is sucked right out of your lungs." Oldfield went on to eat his own words, driving such speed burners as the "Winton Bullet," "Green Dragon," "Blitzen Benz" and "Golden Submarine" to unheard records. In 1909, he took his Benz to the crushed stone and tar surface which now is the site of the Indianapolis Motor Speedway. He drove an average of 83.2 m.p.h. for one mile. This led to the most used phrase of the era by traffic officers—"Who do you think you are going that fast,

Barney Oldfield?" Oldfield's accomplishments led to the resurfacing of the Speedway for the safety and protection of its drivers. They brought in 3.2 million paving bricks. Two years later the Indy 500 was born. The initial winner in 1911 was Ray Harroun. He drove a six-cylinder Marmon Wasp an average of 74.59 m.p.h.

I SHOT AN ARROW INTO THE AIR

Archery is one of the oldest sports known to man. The bow was man's first mechanical invention; the arrow was his first guided missile. The first bow was used between 35,000 and 50,000 years ago and there has never been a period in history since that time in which archers have not been active.

Actually, Robin Hood and his merry men would be no match for the archer of today. For nearly 600 years the English long bow remained unchanged but during the last several years all archery equipment has undergone a revolutionary change. Modern archers with modern equipment are more accurate than any bowmen in history. Bows are faster than ever before. Arrows are high prl a handicap rating from 0 to 10 goals. Ten goals is considered close to perfection. The individual's handicap has nothing to do with his expected scoring in a game. His goal rating is the handicap his team acquires if he participates in their game. The ultimate value of the handicap shows when two teams meet for battle.

Archery as a competitive sport has a history that dates back to the beginning of recorded time. It was a popular sport with the Egyptians, Romans, Greeks, Turks, Mongols and the European nations. In America, the Indians were active in a variety of bow and arrow games.

CHUKKERS, ANYONE?

Polo is probably one of the most evenly balanced of all team sports, due to the handicap system of rating individual players. The system was begun by H. L. Herbert shortly after polo was introduced in America. Every polo player in the country officially engaged in competition receives a handicap rating from 0 to 10 goals. Ten goals is considered close to perfection. The individual's handicap has nothing to do with his expected scoring in a game. His goal rating is the handicap his team acquires if he participates in their game. The ultimate value of the handicap shows when two teams meet for battle.

Each team of four men or women has a team handicap rating: the total of the handicaps of the individual players. When one team's handicap rating is the same as the other's the most equal match should ensue. If a 16 goal team used a 9 goal player, the remaining three players must not exceed the aggregate handicaps of 7 goals. The individual contributions of all four players must be considered in the light of those of the opposing team, position by position. Theoretically, every player prefers a lower rating. With a low rating he is a better benefit to his team if he can play above his handicap.

FOOTBALL OR SOCCER?

Soccer football is played by more people in more countries with more followers than any other game in the world. In international competition and interest it might be argued it eclipses the Olympic Games.

The "World Cup," a true world series of sport, is staged every four years (midway between the Olympic Games) to determine which country can put forth the best national soccer team. To determine the exact world championship team, it permits both the amateur and the professional to play side by side for their country. The FIFA partitions the world into sixteen soccer groups, automatically including the last "World Cup" winner and the hosting nation.

FOR THE BIRDS

Badminton, as presently known, began in England when several local clubs banded together to form the Badminton Association of England. This first national organization helped to establish the rules and regulations, as well as standards for rackets and shuttlecocks, that were necessary before the game could expand internationally. Although the English association did much to spread badminton to other countries, it was as late as 1925 that a touring English group established the game in Canada. In turn the Canadians helped promote badminton in the United States.

The first international match was held in 1902 between England and Ireland. It wasn't until the post World War II years, 1948—49, that the first Thomas Cup Matches were held and badminton reached a truly international competitive state.

Shuttlecocks, commonly referred to as "shuttles" or "birds," are unique objects. When gently tapped, the shuttle flies slower than most objects hit in other sports. But when hit hard, and timed perfectly, the shuttle leaves the racket at a speed of over 110 miles an hour. This range in speed is considered the greatest in any sport for normal play.

THE FOUR FOOTMEN

What was Notre Dame's football record the years the "Four Horsemen" played? Well, the "Four Horsemen," quarterback Harry Stuhldreher, halfbacks Jimmy Crowley and Don Miller and fullback Elmore Layden, played from 1922 to 1924. They actually did not start playing together as a group until the ninth game of their sophomore season of 1922. Layden was shifted from halfback to fullback when Paul Castner suffered a broken leg. They celebrated with a 19-0 victory over Carnegie Tech, and thereafter operated intact throughout their undergraduate days.

They were not dubbed the "Four Horsemen" until the Army game on October 19, 1924, when Grantland Rice gave them that name as they ground out a 13-7 victory. The Irish had a 27-2-1 record during those seasons, playing a scoreless tie with Army in 1922 and losing both games to Nebraska, 14-6 in '22 and 14-7 in '23.

THE BALL OF HISTORY

In the twenty-second chapter of Isaiah is a verse: "He will turn and toss thee like a ball." This allusion indicates that some form of a game with a ball existed as early as 750 B.C. There is evidence that football games were developed and played both in Babylon and early Egypt. In the Sixth Book of Homer's *Odyssey* is a specific allusion to football. "Then having bathed and anointed well with oil they took their mid-day meal upon the river's banks and anon when satisfied with food they played a game of football."

All of the Greek lexicons contain the word *harpaston,* usually defined and described as a game with a ball. References and descriptions of this game identify it as being very similar to modern Rugby football. Harpaston was the early game of Sparta. It was the prime means of training the Spartan warriors. According to original sources it was played on a rectangular field marked with sidelines, goal lines and a center line. There was never any limit to the number of players except that the Greeks insisted that both sides have an equal amount. The purpose of the game was to drive the ball by passing—forward or laterally—kicking or carrying it across the opposite side's goal line. The progress of the ball-carrying side was impeded by blocking, holding and tackling. A prolonged scrimmage ensued without order or method and it was easy to imagine the tremendous stamina which the Spartans had to have.

When the Romans first came into contact with the Greeks they already had a football game of their own called *follis.* Like the phalanx, the Roman game showed more cohesion and teamwork. The Latinization of *harpaston* therefore, was to merge it with *follis.* One of the first acts of Augustus Caesar was to demand the revision of the football rules then in effect. He picked a philosopher and not a gladiator to revise the game. Many detailed descriptions of the Roman game of football, proving its startling similarity to our own game, can be found in the works of Julius Pollux, an Egyptian sophist of the second century A.D.

FAST, FASTER, FASTEST

Jai Alai is sometimes called the fastest sport in the world. The court has three walls and is 180 feet long, 40 feet wide and 40 feet high.

The front wall of the playing court is composed of granite blocks 12 inches thick and the side and back walls of "granite," a pressure-applied cement. Ordinary concrete will slip under the terrific force of the ball which often attains speeds greater than 125 miles an hour. The floor is specially hardened concrete 12 inches thick.

The hand made ball is about three-quarters of the size of a baseball. The core is wound by hand from virgin rubber with a light covering of linen thread which is then covered with goatskin. Because of this special construction the ball is as live as a golf ball and just as hard. The curved basket is strapped to the right hand of the player. The hand is inserted in the glove-like opening at the end of the basket which is then fastened securely to the wrist with a winding of cloth tape. The frame of the basket is painstakingly constructed of thin Spanish chestnut. An imported reed of incredible strength is woven over the frame to provide the ribbed construction so important in putting "spin" on the thrown ball. Each player's basket is tailor made to his special preference in the matter of depth of curve, size, width of opening and balance.

DOWN BUT NOT OUT

Fourteen seconds—the long count—are the most famous in boxing history. On September 22, 1927, a year and a day after they had fought in Philadelphia, Jack Dempsey, now the champion, met once more in Chicago before 104,943 fans.

As before, Tunney was out boxing Dempsey; then, in the seventh round, the challenger caught the champion with a left-right combination and followed it with a barrage that left Tunney seated on his white trunks, with one glove clutching the ropes. Before the bout both fighters had agreed to what was then a new rule: the man scoring a knockdown was required to go immediately to the farthest neutral corner, whereupon the referee would start the count. But Dempsey went to the corner *nearest* the stricken Tunney, while Referee Dave Barry ordered him, at first without effect, to observe the rule. Dempsey finally obeyed and Barry began the count. An instant before he sounded 10, Tunney got to his feet, still shaky and apparently easy prey. But the champion then began a retreat and he weathered the round. He floored Dempsey in the 10th and won the decision.

ON YOUR MARK – PART I

The Olympic Games are of so ancient an origin that they go back beyond the historical era of Greece. Ancient Grecian traditions attributed them to divine origin. The earliest record we have is that of the Olympiad at which Coroebus, the Elean, was victor. That was in 776 B.C. This festival, which continued to be celebrated until 393 A.D., became the basis of the only universally accepted chronological system amoung the Greeks. They counted backward to the Olympics of 776 B.C.; but whether this was really the first Olympiad it is impossible to say. The Greek Games were celebrated in the belief that the spirits of the dead were gratified by such spectacles as delighted them during their earthly life.

During the Homeric age, these festivals were simply sacrifices followed by games at the tomb or before the funeral pyre. Gradually they grew into religious festivals observed by an entire community. Later these festivals—Olympian, Pythian, Nemean, and Isthmian—had attracted wide attention, but the one held at Olympia near the western coast of Greece was by far the most important;, consecrated to the Olympian Zeus. The immediate site of the Games, the Stadium of Olympia, lay towards the northeast of the Altis beyond Mount Kromion. It was an oblong area of about 643 feet in length and about 97 feet wide. It consisted of four sloping heights, two at the sides and two at the ends. The spectators sat on the grassy slopes which accommodated more than 40,000. For the first 13 Olympiads, the competition consisted of a single race of 200 yards. In 708 B.C. the Pentathlon and Wrestling events were introduced; in 688 B.C., Boxing; in 680 the Four Horse Chariot Race; and in 648 the Pancration—a fierce combination of boxing and wrestling. The early rewards were simple crowns of wild olive, but by the 61st Olympiad, it was permitted in Olympia to erect statues in honor of the victors.

During the middle of the second century B.C., Greece came under the domination of the Romans, who permitted the Games to continue although they had little interest in them. Centuries passed. The Games still continued but the high Olympic ideals were entirely discarded and profit alone provided the incentive. In 393 A.D., the Emperor Theodosius forbade the Games altogether, but they had survived a period of nearly 300 Olympiads or approximately 1,200 years.

ON YOUR MARK – PART II

Full credit for the revival of the Olympic Games in the modern era must go to Baron Pierre de Coubertin, who was born in Paris, January 1, 1863, and who died at Geneva, September 2, 1937. Coubertin was not an athlete but he chose athletics as his field. The first major sport with which he associated himself was rowing but when he attempted to bring the British oarsmen to France or send the French oarsmen to compete at Henley, he found the British and French conceptions of amateurism were not the same. This gave him the idea of bringing together educators, diplomats and sports leaders for the purpose of developing a universal understanding of amateurism so that the athletes of all nations might meet on an equal basis. He realized that he would have to originate something spectacular. He began to dream of a revival of the Olympic Games.

At a meeting of the Athletic Sports Union at Sorbonne in Paris, November 25, 1892, Coubertin first publicly announced the Olympic Games idea. However, at this meeting his proposal went for naught. His next opportunity came in the spring of 1894 at an international congress of amateurs. At this meeting, official delegates from France, England, the United States, Greece, Russia, Sweden, Belgium, Italy and Spain were in attendance. Seven questions concerning the problem of amateurism were on the agenda and Coubertin added an eighth, "Regarding the possibility of the revival of the Olympic Games." He imparted his enthusiasm so well that it was unanimously agreed on June 23, 1894, to revive the Games and an International Committee was formed to look after its development and well being. Two years later, in 1896, Greece celebrated, in the rebuilt stadium of Athens, the first Olympic Games of the present cycle.

BASEBALL, BASKETBALL AND FOOTBALL

THROWERS AND STRICKERS

Although the origin of baseball cannot be fixed precisely in time or place, its evolution into its present form is a matter of recorded history. For example: 1835—1840—Because many players were injured by the 4-foot-high stakes which were used as bases the stakes were replaced by flat stones called "stations." The stones were then replaced by sacks filled with sand. Teams had from 11 to 15 players and in some cases as many as 20. 1845—the first game on record to be played under primitive rules was played by a team known as the "Knickerbockers" in Hoboken, New Jersey, who defeated the "New Yorks." The score was 23-1. Alexander Cartwright designed the baseball "diamond," then called a "square." The "thrower's" box was 35 feet from the "striker's" box and the fourth base, now known as home plate. To score a run, a player had to cross the fourth base, which was well to the left of the striker's box. A team of 12 players included an assistant catcher, an infield "rover" and another rover in the outfield. The players were called "scouts." 1857—Nine innings were designated as regulation game; previously a game ended when one team scored 21 runs. 1864—Box score was invented by Henry Chadwick, a baseball writer from Brooklyn. 1867—William Cummings pitched the first "curve." 1875—First glove was worn by Charles C. Waite. And so on.

EVOLUTION

On June 6, 1946, Walter A. Brown, head of the Boston Garden and Al Sutphin of the Cleveland Arena met with other men from other cities for the purpose of founding and promoting a professional basketball league. They called it the Basketball Association of America. At its head was Maurice Podoloff. The BAA began play in the 1946-47 season as a 10 team league in two divisions. More than 25 years later, only two of the original 10 remained—the Boston Celtics and the New York Knickerbockers. From the beginning, the BAA went through two more seasons. There were eight teams in its second season and twelve in its third. Then on August 11, 1949, in Chicago, the BAA merged with the National Basketball League, a 12 year old professional circuit based largely in the Midwest. Together they formed the National Basketball Association with Podoloff as President. The first season saw 17 teams in three divisions. In 1950-51, the NBA became a two division league.

In the years since, the league has added teams and changed rules. One of the most important role changes came about in 1954 when the NBA adopted the 24 second rule. This regulation limited the amount of time a team could hold the ball before taking a shot. Its initial impact was to speed up play, increase the frequency of shooting and to boost scoring totals. When the BAA first began, teams averaged in the neighborhood of 67 points a game. The first season in which the 24 second rule went into effect, team averages jumped 13.5 points a game. One club, the Celtics, finished the season with a mark of 101.4, the first club ever to average more than 100 points a game for a full season. Three years later, every team in the league went over the century mark and it has stayed that way since.

BATS

The most famous of all baseball bats is known as the Louisville Slugger. The origin and development of the firm of Hillerich and Bradsby and its product is a story that could find harmony only against the romantic background of Old Kentucky. J. Frederich Hillerich, born in Baden Baden, Germany, in 1834, emigrated to this country and by 1856 was in business for himself as J. F. Hillerich, Job Turning. In 1880, the owner's son, John Andrew "Bud" Hillerich, 14, started learning his father's trade. One day he was at a baseball game when Pete "The Old Gladiator" Browning, the star slugger of the Eclipse Team (representing Louisville in the old American Association), broke his favorite bat. Browning agreed to accompany Bud to his father's shop after the game. A piece of ash was selected and young Hillerich went to work on it. Pete was right at his side, directing the turning. Many times the bat was removed for testing. Finally Pete pronounced it just right and the next day he got three for three. The Hillerichs were in the bat business, although the father at first resisted the idea.

In 1894, the name Louisville Slugger was registered. One of the policies of the Hillerich & Bradsby Company, as it had been known since 1916, was that sales of bats to players in organized baseball should be made direct to the players. Players began to be exacting in their requirements and records had to be kept of each player's whims and eccentricities and these records could be kept only at the factory.

In 1905, Honus Wagner signed a contract giving J. F. Hillerich and Son permission to use his autograph on Louisville Slugger bats. The idea of using a signature was new at the time. Some of the bat types used by the players were: Eddie Collins, half red and half white timber; Ted Williams, narrow grain pieces; Al Simmons, wide grain. Hugh Duffy's bats had a certain "ring" when bounced on the concrete floor; Ty Cobb's bats came from the same model for 25 years.

THE WEDGE THAT CHANGED IT ALL

It was the flying wedge, football's major offense of 1905, that spurred the formation of the National Collegiate Athletic Association. The rugged nature of the game was causing too many injuries and deaths. Many institutions discontinued the sport. Others advocated that it be abolished from the intercollegiate program. In early December, 1905, Chancellor H. M. MacCracken of New York University, called a meeting of 13 colleges and universities to bring about reforms in football playing rules. Earlier, President Theodore Roosevelt had summoned college athletic leaders to two White House conferences to urge reformation of the game. At a subsequent meeting December 28 in New York City, the Intercollegiate Athletic Association was founded by 62 colleges and universities. The Association was officially constituted March 31, 1906, and the NCAA took its present name in 1910.

THE BABE

The first game Babe Ruth played in professional baseball was as pitcher for the Baltimore Orioles of the International League in 1914. While only 200 fans attended the game, the Babe shut out the Buffalo Bisons 6-0. He also shut out Joe McCarthy, who was to be his manager in later years as a Yankee and who that day was playing second base for Buffalo. Ruth hit the clock in center field for two bases and got another blow besides.

As a big leaguer the Babe pitched two opening games and won them both. In the first, at Fenway Park in 1916, he beat the Athletics, 2-1. The next year he beat the Yankees at the Polo Grounds 10-3, with three hits. When the Babe made the transition from left-handed pitcher to outfielder, he wasted no time in slamming a homer in the opening game of the 1919 season. Two years later, as a Yankee, he kept an opening crowd at the Polo Grounds in constant uproar with a bombardment of two doubles and three singles in five trips to the plate.

One of the biggest occasions in baseball was the opening of the Yankee Stadium on April 18, 1923. The new park, then baseball's grandest, was packed with celebrities, including Governor Alfred E. Smith and Mayor John F. Hylan. More than 60,000 fans poured into the shiny new park. Ruth proceeded to take charge in the third inning when he pigeon-toed up to the plate and slammed a slow curve into the right field stand for a homer. The Yanks won, 4-1. Thus did Babe christen "The House That Ruth Built."

THE GIPPER

It was in the 1940 film classic *Knute Rockne* that Ronald Reagan and Pat O'Brien, playing George Gipp and Knute Rockne, were featured in the now famous tearjerking scene: it occurs when Gipp, the Irish halfback, looks up from his hospital bed and gazes wearily into the baby blue eyes of O'Brien, portraying Notre Dame's immortal football coach. Gipp was on his deathbed after having been clipped by a streptococcic infection of the throat. A voice from behind Rockne whispered, "It's pretty tough to go."

What's tough about it?" Gipp asked with a weak smile. Then he turned to Rockne. "Rock," he said, "I've got to go. It's all right. Some time, Rock, when the team is up against it, when things are wrong and the breaks are beating the boys, tell them to go in there with all they've got and win just for the Gipper. I don't know where I'll be then, Rock, but I'll know about it. And I'll be happy."

Then the legendary Gipper died.

In real life Rockne retold Gipp's death message to his players only once. That was in a game when Army held the upper hand over the Fighting Irish at halftime. During the intermission Rockne's talk about the Gipper was an inspiring oratory. The Irish players came back breathing fire and won the game on the late Jack Chevigny's touchdown. After Chevigny finally was stopped in the end zone, he made the classic statement, "That's one for the Gipper."

George Gipp never played high school football. He went to Notre Dame to play baseball. One day Rockne saw him punting a ball 70 yards and he was soon in a freshman football uniform. When Gipp was in his prime, Notre Dame won 19 and tied one, scoring 506 points to the opposition's 97. Gipp was Notre Dame's first All-American, and according to Rockne, he was the greatest halfback who ever represented the school.

PEACH BASKETS

Basketball was invented in December 1891 by Dr. James A. Naismith, a Canadian clergyman, who was a student instructor at the international Young Men's Christian Association Training School, Springfield, Massachusetts. It was the only major sport originated and developed in the United States.

At the YMCA in Springfield, Naismith was given the task of inventing a recreative game which could be played indoors during the winter months. At first he tried to modify some of the existing out-of-doors games, but he found none suitable for indoor play. He then started with the principle that a game in which a ball could be thrown but not carried would eliminate objectionable roughness. Next he decided on some sort of a target or goal. This meant a horizontal goal, so placed that a curve would be necessary for a successful score and high enough so that the defense would not congregate around it. Shouldering, pushing and kicking were prohibited by the rules. Two wooden peach baskets were chosen as goals and hung at each end of the gymnasium and a soccer ball was selected as the closest among existing balls to what was needed.

From the very first day as it was played among the eighteen members of Naismith's gymnasium class, basketball has been popular. In comparison to many sports very few basic rule changes have been made throughout the years.

DOUBLE PLAY

Tinker to Evers to Chance has become synonymous with the double play. However, comparison of double plays now being made with the so-called lively ball far outshines any of the old time records. In 1906, as the Chicago Cubs drove to their first pennant, they managed exactly eight double plays that went Tinker to Evers to Chance. A year later the Cubs won another pennant and made seven double plays that went the same route. And in 1908, when the cubs won for the third straight time, there were just eight more made by the same combination. Over the three years the Cubs were, of course, in three World Series. In all they played 16 series games. In all 16 games there were no Tinker-to-Evers-to-Chance double plays. This fact may be partly explained by the following: 1906-1908 was the era of the dead ball and it was far more difficult to execute a double play than it is today when the lively ball rockets off the bat and is fielded before the hitter is well out of the batter's box. In comparison some of today's teams are executing double plays in the hundreds for a season.

GAMES

THE QUIET GAME

Early in the eighteenth century two young monks who had disobeyed orders were placed in seclusion for three months—under the rule of silence. During their idle hours they gathered and numbered twenty-eight stones. Although it was difficult to communicate without speaking, after several days they had managed to invent a game.

When one was victor his excitement was great but *the* rule of silence could not be broken. So the moment a game was won, the victor uttered the first line of the prayer: *"Dixit Dominum Domino* Meo.*"*

The game was soon adopted by other inhabitants of the monastery as a lawful pastime, and as years passed, it spread from village to town and finally around the world. The prayer by which the winner signaled victory was shortened to one word, known today as—Domino!

THE ROBOT

No one knows how chess originated but it is mentioned in Hindu literature of at least 3,000 years before Christ. It spread through Burma to Tibet, Siam and China and was taken from China to Japan. It came westward through Constantinople, probably around the sixth century. It subsequently spread through Europe by way of the Danube River.

In the eighteenth century, Europe was fascinated and puzzled for more than fifty years by an invention called Kempelen's Chess Player, an automaton. The public could hardly believe that a mechanical man could play chess so well it frequently beat the best players of the time. Suspicion that the legless figure contained a human being was largely dispelled by the fact that it had little doors that could be opened to view its working machinery and also by the knowledge that no midget or person without legs traveled with Kempelen. But it did contain a legless man who wore artificial limbs in public and was never suspected of being a cripple.

HOLY POKER

The first rules for whist were formulated and published by the Englishman Edmond Hoyle (1672-1769). This started the expression "according to Hoyle." Although the phrase has made his name proverbial as an authority on all games, most of those played today were invented after his death, including pinochle and poker.

History has recorded many classic poker games, but one with a unique twist occurred near the turn of the century in the rough frontier of Cody, Wyoming. One evening a group of local men, including Colonel William F. Cody (Buffalo Bill) and Governor Beck of Wyoming, were enjoying a friendly game. As the pot grew larger Colonel Cody suggested that since the game was for pleasure, no one man should win such a sum as that on the table. It was agreed that the lucky gentleman would give the money toward a new church. Governor Beck won the stakes and immediately proclaimed that an Episcopal church would be built. Meantime the ladies of the community gave dinners and held bazaars until a sum as large as the one donated by the poker players had been collected. Christ Church was built and consecrated in 1902. In 1942, when the church observed its fortieth anniversary, Governor Beck was present to tell about the poker game which provided the first funds for the church building.

WHAT ABOUT "OQU"

Roque is a form of croquet, but it requires a much greater degree of skill. A perfectly smooth dirt court is needed and a very slightly sloping surface to carry away the water. Composition balls course across this smooth surface like ivory balls on a billiard table. All around the court runs a bank made of heavy timbers or of cement, against which the balls rebound. Delicate carom shots are often made on these banks. The arches used in roque are three and three-eighths inches wide, which is just one-eighth inch wider than the diameter of the balls. The mallets have short handles and sometimes are bound with brass to prevent splitting. One end is often tipped with rubber.

The game of roque was given its name by Jared S. Babcock of New York, who evolved it by the simple expedient of omitting the first and last letters from the word "croquet," making a word of one syllable.

MISCELLANEOUS

SPASMS, FRECKLES AND LUMPS

What makes our teeth chatter? Why do some of us have freckles? What causes a lump in a person's throat?

When a person is cold, he is apt to have a spasm of shivering over which his brain does not seem to have any control. The spasm causes the muscles of the jaw to contract very quickly, and soon as they are extracted, they let the jaw fall again of its own weight. This spasm-and-relaxation pattern, occurring many times in rapid succession, causes the teeth to chatter. There are two kinds of spasms, clonic and tonic. In the former the muscles contract and relax alternately in very quick succession, producing an appearance of agitation. In the latter the muscles contract in a steady, uniform manner and remain contracted for a comparatively long time.

Some people have freckles while others do not because all skins are not alike, just as all eyes are not the same color. People with certain kinds of skin freckle more quickly with exposure to the sun. The action of the sun causes small parts of the second layer of skin to give out a yellow or yellowish brown substance. Freckles are most common in persons with fair complexion and hair.

When someone eats something, it passes into his throat after he has chewed it and a 9 inches or l0 inches series of rings passes or squeezes it from one set of muscle rings to the next. These muscle rings can move the food both up and down: if something is eaten that causes vomiting, the muscles work backwards and force the matter from the stomach. When one is frightened, a hollow sensation is felt in the stomach and the throat muscles work upward, pressing against the windpipe and causing one to feel as if there was a lump.

THE TRADEMARK

Names and symbols were applied to products by guilds of the Middle Ages. But the legal right to limit the use of such marks is a modern development.   In the middle 1700s, English courts ruled that the trademark did not exist as we know it today. If one man could use it, anyone could use it. The first attempt by the English courts to keep one person from using another's trademark was in 1803. In the United States, the first federal law for the registration of trademarks was passed in 1870. It was declared unconstitutional. The present law, more limited in purpose, was passed in 1905 and has been amended several times.

CITY PLANNERS

City development and planning during the Middle Ages often seemed haphazard. This was not necessarily true. The streets of most medieval towns were narrow and the towns were small and close-knit because of the need for protection against the dangers of the times. Irregular yet carefully developed public squares, bordered by the church and the city hall, were the central features.

Sometimes a town would be moved to an entirely new site in order to improve its commercial advantages or health conditions. Examples of this are Salisbury, England; Lubeck, Germany and Bilboa, Spain. New towns were also built by noblemen as centers of administration, buffers against hostile powers or places to enforce rule in remote areas. The French towns known as *bastides* such as Monpazier and Aigues-Mortes were of this type.

During the Renaissance and baroque period increased interest in symmetry, perspective and order in city planning developed. The Spaniards in South America built towns to a rigidly specified gridiron pattern. In North America the cities of Philadelphia and Savannah were built in a rectilinear design.

SLOW DOWN

As far back as 3000 B.C. there were traffic signs. Inscribed stones marked the trade routes across Persia, Arabia and what is today Afghanistan. The Phoenicians used basalt obelisks for the same purpose. When the Romans built their 50,000 mile network of paved roads linking the empire, stone arrows inset in the road guided the traveler to his destination. Signs warned him of driving restrictions. Signs were used to direct one-way traffic in the business parts of the capital city's narrow streets.

In the United States, Providence, Rhode Island, probably posted the first speed limit sign in 1690, after a horseman ran down a child. Boston had speed signs in 1750. But outside the cities, road markers were practically unknown. When the covered wagons pushed westward across the Alleghenys and followed the buffalo trails across the great plains and the western mountains, a piece of cloth hung on a branch or a crude arrow on the ground served to mark the route for following wagons.

It was not until the motor car came into use about the turn of the last century that traffic signs similar to those we know today came into being. New York City posted its first speed limit sign—10 miles an hour—in 1900, and in 1903 erected what may have been the first regulatory signs. These were 100 blue and white enameled signs notifying slow moving traffic to keep near the curb.

Massachusetts had signs at all road intersections by 1912, but they were small and hard to read. In most of the country, the only route markers were crude, homemade signs with directions to the next town that were put up by local authorities or by some farmer who grew tired of being asked for road directions. Private companies began installing signs that combined road information with an advertising message. By 1912 one tire company claimed it had put up such signs on more than 20,000 miles of roads from Maine to California and Canada to Mexico. Automobile clubs in the larger cities undertook broad scale road signing programs as a service to their members.

IT'S IN THE NAME

When Susie Jones gets a job in the movies the studio bills her as the glamorous Cicely Morrow. During the long career the public knows her by no other name.

But consider the name Wedgwood, widely known for a particular type of high quality pottery. Not only would the family resist changing the name but would sue other manufacturers seeking to capitalize on its use.

The first known Wedgwood potter was Gilbert Wedgwood who, in 1649, was making pots at the Churchyard Works, Burslem, England. In 1759, his great-great-grandson, Josiah Wedgwood, founded the present business, conducted by his direct descendants. Etruria, the factory he built in 1769, was superseded in 1938-40 by a new one at Barlaston, five miles from Stoke-on-Trent. To this new factory went the priceless stock of designs and molds—some going back to the eighteenth century—many of which are still in use today.

Wedgwood bone china has some advantage over continental or feldspar porcelain. It is stronger, whiter, more translucent, has a more brilliant glaze and it can be decorated with a greater variety of brighter colors. The word Wedgwood can only be applied to ware made by Josiah Wedgwood and Sons Limited. The trademark Wedgwood has been incorporated into the backstamps on all Wedgwood ware since the last quarter of the eighteenth century. Other pottery manufacturers have used the word Wedgwood in their names but in actuality have no connection with the original Wedgwood or their products. In recent years legal action has been taken against several other manufacturers by Josiah Wedgwood & Sons Ltd., in the use of the name.

PANIC ON THE AIRWAYS

According to the *New York Times* of October 31, 1938, one radio broadcast achieved a result just south of bedlam:

:   "A wave of mass hysteria seized thousands of radio listeners throughout the nation last night when a broadcast of H. G. Well's fantasy, *The War of the Worlds,* led thousands to believe than an interplanetary conflict had started with invading Martians spreading wide death and destruction in :New Jersey and New York."

The broadcast, which disrupted households, interrupted religious services, created traffic jams and clogged communication systems, was made by Orson Welles, who as the radio character, "The Shadow," used to give "the creeps" to countless child listeners. This time, at least a score of adults required medical treatment for shock and hysteria.

In Newark, in a single block—more than twenty families rushed out of their houses with wet handkerchiefs and towels over their faces to flee what they believed was to be a gas raid. Some began moving household furniture.

Throughout New York, families left their homes, some to flee to nearby parks. Thousands of persons called the police, newspapers and radio stations here and in other cities of the United States and Canada seeking advice or protective measures against the raids.

The memory of that hoax was still so vivid in the minds of many listeners that three years later hundreds of them refused to believe the first radio reports of the bombing of Pearl Harbor.

THE ELECTRIC BODY

During the coming year hundreds of people will die by accidental electrocution in the United States. However, electrocutions only account for about one percent of the total number of accidental deaths. In a way, this is surprising, for electricity is potentially the most dangerous product in use by the general public.

The intricate nerve structure of the human body makes man very sensitive to even small amounts of electric current. Just as the nerves react to intense heat and subzero temperature, they also respond to electric stimulation. Electricity affects the muscles as well as the nerves, causing the muscles to contract or become paralyzed. Severe electric shock can affect the heart and other vital organs.

Some parts of the body are more sensitive than others to electricity. The tongue, for example, can detect an almost negligible amount of current—from 45 millionths of an ampere when platinum wires are energized and held firmly against it. The body reacts to shock in many ways. Currents only slightly greater than those that are barely perceptible cause muscular contraction, heat and pain. When currents of about 10 to 10 thousandths of an ampere flow through the hand, an involuntary muscular reaction takes place which is said to "freeze" the victim to the circuit. Such currents are in excess of what is known as the "let go" limit, the maximum current which a person can withstand without loss of normal muscular control. In experiments it has been found that the average "let go" limit is just under 17 milliamperes for men and 10 1/2 milliamperes for women.

One of the serious effects of electric shock is respiratory paralysis, caused when current flows through the respiratory nerves located at the base of the brain and in the chest area. This results in a nerve block, cutting off nerve impulses to the respiratory muscles. In the absence of normal communications between nerves and respiratory muscles, breathing is interrupted for a considerable length of time. Artificial respiration on the part of the rescuer can often prevent fatal results.

SOUTHPAWS

Scientists have found left-handed snails, left-handed flounders and even left-handed trees. But none of these diverse forms of life has problems as complex as those which may confront the left-handed child.

In primitive societies, the left-handed child was often regarded as ill-starred and unlucky. Among the Kafir tribes of Southern Africa, parents of a left-handed infant sometimes scalded the left hand with hot sand to induce the youngster to use the other. In New Zealand, the Maoris disliked the left hand and used it as little as possible. Something of this feeling persists even today in our language. The word *sinister* comes from the Latin, and its primary meaning is simply "left" or "toward the left side." By contract, the Latin word for the right side is *dexter,* which has given us the approving word *dexterous.*

Parents may still regard their left-handed offspring somewhat ruefully, and with some justification, for the ordinary right-handed world makes very little special provision for the southpaw. The chances are he'll go through life fumbling with right-handed pencil sharpeners and telephone dials and bumping elbows with his dinner companions. And, he may feel a bit awkward when he starts learning to dance.

Musical instruments offer another pitfall to the left-handed youngster. The piano, for example, is a right-handed instrument, that is, the more difficult and intricate passages are played with the right hand. A left-handed violinist might have less difficulty, assuming that he had a left-handed violin, but if he played in the string section of a symphony orchestra, they'd have to make a little extra room for him.

THE FICKLE FINGER

Alphonse Bertillon, director of the Identity Department of the French Prefecture of Police is credited with being the first detective who caught a killer by means of fingerprints, but it was Sir Francis Galton, the English scientist-physician, who found that every person's fingerprints are unique. Galton's radical new system of identification was in workable and virtually finished form by 1892. However, it was generally agreed at that time that no jury would ever convict a man of a serious offense on such flimsy evidence.

In 1902, a burglar broke into the home of a Parisian dentist and was discovered by a servant. In the ensuing struggle the servant was killed. Assigned to the case Bertillon collected bits of broken glass found at the scene of the crime. One fragment showed four fingerprints. They led the detective to a professional criminal who was an enemy of the dead man. On the basis of fingertip identification, the killer was convicted and fingerprinting spread throughout the world.

MAIL DELIVERY

The postage stamp arose from the custom of sending packages and mail from post to post. One messenger carried the mail to a certain post or station, where it was picked up by another messenger who carried it to another station. The work "postage" meant the charge for carrying mail. The sender of the letter or package sealed it with wax and stamped the wax with a seal or ring bearing his signature, giving rise to the term "stamp." At first the mail was carried by private couriers and the charge was based on the number of sheets in a letter and the distance it had to travel.

In the 1830s, an Englishman named Rowland Hill suggested that stamps should be used on mail and that the cost of the mail should be determined by the weight. In 1840, Great Britain started to issue postage stamps. It was the first country to do so and the idea spread rapidly. Zurich and Geneva were the next to issue postage stamps. Brazil issued stamps in 1843. Some private letter carrying services in the United States were issuing stamps in 1843 before the government took over the mails.

There were many post offices in the United States that were located in difficult to reach places. The federal government made contracts with private messengers for the delivery of mail to such offices. The messenger guaranteed to pick up mail and deliver it by the swiftest, safest means possible. His route was known as a star route, because post-office records indicated such routes with three stars, or asterisks which stood for celerity, certainty and security. Star route service is not the same as rural free delivery. This is taken care of by civil service employees. Star routes became less important as railroads were built throughout the country, but when automobiles began to be widely used, railroads stopped serving many places and the number of star routes increased.